PRIMARY FOUNDATIONS

PSHE and citizenship

AGES 5-7

Judith Hill

CONTENTS

Author
Judith Hill

Editor
Clare Gallaher

Assistant Editor
Keith Hutchings

Series designer
Lynne Joesbury

Designer
Anna Oliwa

Illustrations
Ray and Corinne Burrows

Cover photograph
Digital Vision

Published by
Scholastic Ltd,
Villiers House,
Clarendon Avenue,
Leamington Spa,
Warwickshire
CV32 5PR
Printed by Bell & Bain Ltd, Glasgow
Text © 2001 Judith Hill © 2001 Scholastic Ltd

4 5 6 7 8 9 0
4 5 6 7 8 9 0

Visit our website at
www.scholastic.co.uk

British Library Cataloguing-in-Publication Data
A catalogue record for this book is available from
the British Library.

ISBN 0-439-01857-9

The right of Judith Hill to be identified as the Author of this work has been asserted by her in accordance with the Copyright, Designs and Patents Act 1988.

Introduction

This book suggests how PSHE and citizenship can be divided into manageable teaching units for five- to seven-year-olds. Each themed chapter provides two units of work. These units are often complementary to each other and therefore you should choose one or other as appropriate to your needs. Most of the units can be used to form the basis of a substantial chunk of personal, social and health education work – perhaps over half a term – and, by providing progressive lesson plans, show how PSHE and citizenship can be sequenced. The grids at the beginning of each unit are intended to aid medium-term planning. They highlight (in bold) the enquiry questions covered by the lesson plans as well as additional enquiry questions which could be used to extend the unit further. The grids can also be used to help plan links that PSHE and citizenship has with other subjects across the curriculum, especially literacy. (ICT links are given within the lesson plans themselves.) By providing a broad overview, the grids also help with planning the resources that you will need to collect in preparation for the unit.

The introductions to each unit provide some background information that you may find useful when working with the lesson plans. There is also guidance provided on matching learning opportunities to a range of ability levels.

Renewing an old debate

There has long been a debate about the precise nature and contribution of PSHE and citizenship to the curriculum. Within schools you would be unlikely to find disagreement over the basic need for the curriculum to promote the spiritual, moral, cultural, mental and physical development of children as well as preparing them for the opportunities, responsibilities and experiences of adult life. Indeed, schools are required to include these areas in their curriculum. Neither, one suspects, would there be much disagreement over the essential ingredients of that programme. Instead much of the debate has been focused on issues of where to fit the provision within the existing curriculum structure and, equally importantly, what teaching methods and approaches to employ. Increasing pressures and demands from other areas of the curriculum have meant that difficult decisions about priorities have had to be made. The non-statutory guidance in the National Curriculum (2000) goes some way in answering some of these questions by providing a model which demonstrates progression, continuity and breadth of opportunity. This book has taken these guidelines as its basis and shown how manageable units of work can result from them.

Why is PSHE and citizenship important?

There are a number of good reasons that support the inclusion of personal, social and health education and citizenship in the school curriculum. The first is that children are entitled to an education which includes a personal and social dimension in much the same way as they have an entitlement to the provision of literacy and numeracy. Such a provision recognises the need for children to understand and appreciate fully the basis of human and interpersonal behaviour and how this affects the individual, the group and the community as a whole. This will enable children to have the confidence and independence that will help them to become informed and responsible citizens.

A second fundamental part of this provision is that it contributes to the development of children's social and interpersonal skills. These skills will enable them to interrelate effectively with their peer group, with parents and teachers, and with other adults. They will also be made more aware of their own worth as individuals.

The final benefit that this entitlement offers is the opportunity to hold an open and honest exploration of individual and community attitudes, values and beliefs within a safe and supportive environment. This will help children to assess their responsibilities and rights as members of a community and to appreciate diversity and differences between individuals.

To sum up, PSHE and citizenship is important because it helps children to develop mutual respect and support for each other; it encourages them to make informed decisions about issues discussed; it supports the learning skills of life, such as:
● awareness of and care for others and the environment
● learning to state effectively one's own feelings
● being constructively critical and questioning
● being responsible for one's own behaviour and learning.

PSHE and citizenship in school and the community
Within the 'community' of the school, there is a need for understanding of the importance of good social and interpersonal skills. These are the essential building blocks for creating a supportive learning environment. Effective and meaningful relationships between the children themselves and between the children and the staff lie at the heart of an 'achieving' school.

Parents and carers are also a part of that community, and the development of children's social and interpersonal skills is perceived by many parents to be a key responsibility of the school. At the same time, many people would regard this as a goal only achievable through a genuine partnership between home and school.

The community, in its wider context of the society in which we live, frequently expresses its shock and outrage at some of the extreme antisocial behaviour of certain individuals and groups. There is often a sense that society is entitled to better standards of behaviour, but this is often accompanied by a lack of understanding of how this might be achieved.

PSHE and citizenship for five- to seven-year-olds
In this book the themes reflect the areas that have been highlighted in the National Curriculum non-statutory guidelines on PSHE and citizenship. These provide an appropriate context to explore social and interpersonal issues, including health, environment and relationships. Each unit begins by establishing what the children already know and understand about the topics. They are encouraged to build up their knowledge through various experiences and exchanges with their peer group, family and friends. A range of approaches is used to promote understanding, including stories, role-play and art, and suggestions for discussion and debate are provided.

Each unit identifies general and specific skills related to the theme and begins by allowing the children to 'audit' their own skills as a basis for building further competencies. All activities have a skill-building component, and also allow for the exploration and examination of personal values and beliefs. Within the themes, children can explore their own personal expectations as they relate to some of these important issues. They will also be given opportunities to consider the expectations of others, whether they be friends, family or the wider community.

Building healthy relationships

The personal and social development of children in the early years of primary school constitutes a major consideration for teachers, parents and others who share the responsibility for this crucial stage of their development. These children are embarking on a period of significant change in their lives, and it is a time when their interaction with other children and adults will increase rapidly.

Whatever the nature of personal and social pre-school experiences children may have had, opportunities for them to be given individual attention will decrease. Having to learn to share their teacher's attention with many other children as well as learning to collaborate with their peer group as part of a much larger community constitutes a steep learning curve for many children of this age group. They have to come to terms relatively quickly with some of the wider complexities of social and personal relationships. They will become increasingly aware of the fact that they will not always be at the centre of other people's attention. They will begin to learn that their requests, whether polite or otherwise, will not always be met with an immediate response; in some cases – not at all.

As children begin to integrate and grow within the school community, their perceptions of personal relationships change. Many friendships at the start of school life are influenced by parental choice, demography and other pre-school experiences, such as playgroup and nursery. Gradually, school gives children the opportunity to choose their own friends for the first time. The qualities of what constitutes a friend move from those that satisfied their early egocentric needs to a wider appreciation and understanding of the importance of character and personality in developing and sustaining friendships. Equally, they will begin to appreciate that friendships can be transient and will have to learn to cope with the ever-changing nature of relationships.

Contexts for developing young children's social awareness

The National Curriculum framework for PSHE and citizenship emphasises the importance of children learning about themselves as developing individuals and as members of their communities. Within the context of the classroom and home, and with reference to things and people that are within their personal experience, children should be given the opportunity to explore and share what and who are special to them.

Through a range of teacher-led discussion and paired and group activities in this chapter, children are encouraged to develop their own self-awareness and self-esteem and value their individual qualities. They are also encouraged to explore personal feelings and emotions as a form of response to situations. The activities help the children to think about the qualities of others and to understand how relationships are developed and sustained. Through class and small group discussion, they are also encouraged to learn about other people's feelings and to develop an awareness of the views, needs and rights of other children and adults.

The main areas explored within this chapter are the concept of 'special'; making, breaking and mending relationships; the importance of memory in the development of a positive self-image; responsibilities towards other people.

CHAPTER I

Being special

The concept of 'special' in this unit focuses specifically on the value and significance of the individual experiences, understanding and awareness of children during their early years in school. Children of this age begin to form an understanding of the word *special* at varying levels and in a variety of contexts. Equally, they begin to appreciate that others may interpret the word differently from them.

The aims of the unit are therefore to encourage children to identify and assess their own experiences of what is special as they relate to personal feelings, emotions and relationships. In so doing, they will gain an appreciation of their own worth and recognise the positive qualities of those around them. At the same time, they are helped to understand what the term can mean to other people.

This unit allows children to explore a range of attitudes and values, which is achieved by:
- encouraging them to reflect on personal characteristics and qualities
- helping them to explore personal strengths and weaknesses
- encouraging them to grow in self-confidence and develop a positive self-image
- helping them to recognise and deal with their feelings in a positive way
- encouraging them to set simple goals
- helping them to appreciate the opinions and feelings of others close to them.

The structure of each activity within the unit allows children to take part in discussions within a large or small group, share ideas and feelings in a 'safe' environment, and think about themselves and learn from their experiences.

Through carrying out the activities, the children can explore the idea of being 'special'. Using a range of contexts and specific curriculum areas, such as literacy, art and technology, the children can investigate and report on their personal learning. They can be stimulated into considering, sharing and reviewing their experiences and their understanding. They can be provided with additional insights and perspectives that build on and enhance their understanding.

Although each activity can stand alone, there is progression built into the structure of the unit so that assessment of previous learning objectives can be achieved through questioning during the introduction of the next activity. Depending on the age and ability of children in the class, it may be possible to develop learning which considers more complex ideas associated with qualities, attitudes and values.

Displays of key vocabulary, previous learning, children's work and other visual stimuli are an important part of the unit as they enable children to recall experiences and ideas previously shared, and also give them the opportunity to celebrate what they have discovered about themselves.

As in all discussion of aspects of personal, social and emotional development, it is important to recognise issues relating to individual children. In particular, you need to be sensitive to children with low self-esteem and to those who have had to be separated, whether temporarily or permanently, from a member of their family. Equally, relationships within the peer group will require sensitive handling for some children, particularly those who find such relationships difficult to establish and maintain.

UNIT: Being special

Enquiry questions	Learning objectives	Teaching activities	Learning outcomes	Cross-curricular links
What is special to me?	• Recognise what they like and that things are special for a variety of reasons. • Learn that things that are special to them require their care and respect. • Understand that other people's ideas of what *they* regard as special must be treated with respect.	Group reading of a story about a special object. Teacher-led discussion about objects that are special to the children. Paired discussions about special objects, followed by labelling objects for display, and writing and drawing about them.	Children: • understand the concept of 'special' and express their ideas with confidence • appreciate that something that is valued is not necessarily worth a lot of money • talk about their feelings and emotions in relation to the idea of something special	English: presenting own thoughts and feelings about an object to an audience; focusing on descriptive words. Art and design: drawing 'special' objects.
Who are my special people?	• Think about how most of the people who are special to them love and care for them. • Understand that they can make special people happy or sad.	Whole-class discussion about people who are special in the children's lives. Group activities: making zigzag books; constructing model figures; writing key phrases about a special person.	• extend their understanding of 'special' to people rather than things • appreciate that how people treat us affects how we feel about them • understand the impact of other people's behaviour on them as well as the impact of their behaviour on others	Science: recognising the main external parts of the human body.
Why are people special?	• Recognise that they belong to various groups and communities, such as the school community. • Understand that the skills and qualities of people within their immediate community and outside play a role in their own welfare and development. • Realise that the individual's contribution is important for the whole community. • Learn how to set simple goals.	Teacher-led discussion about people who are special in the local community and the wider world. A visit from a person who has a special role to play in the community. Individual or paired activities: creating a poster in which a person who has special qualities is sought.	• understand the distinction between skills and qualities • appreciate the special contribution that individuals can make to their community • make the link between what people do and how it affects their own lives	History: learning about the lives of significant people in the past.
How am I special?	• Recognise and value their own special qualities and appreciate that those of others are important. • Respect the differences between people.	Whole-class discussion which focuses on appreciating the differences between people. Group activity with recording of children's responses. Individuals completing starter sentences.	• recognise and value their own qualities • recognise and value the qualities of others • respect the differences between others and appreciate that people are special in different ways	English: reading stories which celebrate differences between people.
What do other people think about me?	• Think about themselves, learn from other people's opinions of themselves and recognise what they are good at.	Re-enactment of a *This is Your Life* television show. Children taking it in turns to present interesting facts about individuals in the class.	• are confident and show support of each other	English: describing events and experiences; speaking to different people, including friends, the class, teachers and other adults.
Which places are special to me?	• Realise that different places in the environment are very important to different people. • Understand that feelings are hurt when a person's place that is special to them is damaged in some way.	Teacher-led discussion about special places in stories and in the children's own lives. Compiling a Big Book of children's drawings and writing about special places.	• show an appreciation of what makes different places special for different reasons • appreciate that other people have different special places • express their feelings about sharing their special place or it being damaged.	English: reading about places that are significant in particular stories. Geography: knowledge and understanding of places.

50 mins What is special to me?

Learning objectives
● Recognise what they like and that things are special for a variety of reasons.
● Learn that things that are special to them require their care and respect.
● Understand that other people's ideas of what *they* regard as special must be treated with respect.

Lesson organisation
Whole-class story and discussion; individual and paired activities; plenary.

Vocabulary
special
valued
worth
care
favourite
treasure
precious

What you need and preparation

Before the activity, explain to the children that you are going to make a collection of special things, and that you would like them to bring in one item of their choice to school, for example, a toy, a book, a photograph, a box or tin, something they found on holiday. (Remind them to ask permission at home to do this.) Gather together some of your own 'special' things which could also be referred to in the discussion, for example something old (a photograph album, a favourite book from your childhood, a piece of jewellery belonging to your grandmother) and something new (an object that has recently become important in some way, a special award).

Prepare a display area in advance, where the special objects can be put on view, once they have been discussed in the activity. You will also need: photocopiable pages 107 and 108; board or flip chart; blank labels; key words on cards (for less confident children); paper; writing, colouring and drawing materials.

What to do

20 mins Introduction

Introduce the idea of having something which we regard as special or precious. Read the story of 'The squirrel in the garden' on photocopiable page 107 to the children. Discuss the most important features of the story, for example the way in which the squirrel took trouble to avoid anyone seeing what he had or what he was doing. Do the children know what was special to the squirrel? Emphasise the concept of a special object, possession or prize.

Ask the children to place their special objects on the table in front of them. Can they describe one way in which they behave towards their object which shows that it is special? For example, keeping it in a safe place and being extra careful not to lose it. Invite individual children to tell the rest of the class about why their objects are special, and record key points on the board.

Now show your own possessions to the children and discuss them, explaining why they are special to you. Draw out key vocabulary related to the idea of something special – *favourite*, *valued* and so on – asking the children:
● Can you think of other words for *special*?
● How often can you remember using the word *special*?
● When you used it last time, what did you use it to describe?
● Is *special* the same as *favourite*?

Focusing on their own objects again, finish the discussion by asking them:
● What makes your object a special thing for you? (Introduce the idea that *special* does not always mean 'expensive', 'worth a lot of money'.)
● Why do you think different people find different objects special to them?

20 mins Development

Organise the children into pairs to talk for a few minutes about their special object with their

partner. Encourage them to discuss things like why it is special, how they got it and where they keep it. Distribute some blank labels and invite them to make a label for their object. These can then be used for the display.

Provide each child with a copy of photocopiable page 108 and ask them to colour in the star shape that most closely describes their special object. Encourage them to draw their object on a separate sheet of paper, then use their own words to describe it. They can then colour in the appropriate box for *I like to...* before completing the starter sentences in question 5.

10 **Plenary**
mins Ask a pair of children or an individual from each table to share what they have written. Ask the rest of the class for their thoughts on the ideas that have been presented. Do they feel the same way as one another? Discuss key points that arise.

Invite the children to talk about what they thought was the most important part of the activity. What was the most interesting or unusual thing they heard or found out about?

Differentiation

Less able children may need help with understanding the categories in the boxes given in the first question on the photocopiable sheet. Provide them with a list of key words to choose from to help them describe their special thing (question 3). Make sure that they have adult support to complete question 5, or ask them to work in pairs to share their ideas. Encourage more able children to extend their ideas when they are writing their sentences for question 5.

Assessing learning outcomes

Do the children understand the concept of 'special' and are they able to express their ideas about what they like with confidence? Do they appreciate that something that is valued may not necessarily be worth a great deal of money? Are they able to talk about their feelings and emotions in relation to the idea of something special?

ICT opportunities
The children could word-process their own labels for the display of special objects and also key in a list of descriptive words for each object.

Follow-up activities
● Ask the children to draw another two objects that are special to them.
● Make a class poster which contains statements about how the children feel if things that are special to them get lost or broken.
● Talk about special occasions and invite the children to draw their own special occasion. They could add labels that highlight the 'special' features.

1 hour 15 mins Who are my special people?

What you need and preparation

Collect one or two posters showing photographs of family members and other groups which can be used to discuss the theme of special people. Before the activity, invite the children to bring in photographs from home that are of people who are close to them. You will also need: large strips of paper or card made up into blank four-page zigzag books; various sizes of card cut into the shapes of different body parts; paper fasteners; small clothes made out of card (optional); board or flip chart; glue (optional); large sheets of paper; small pieces of card; writing, colouring and drawing materials.

What to do
20 **Introduction**
mins Begin with a whole-class discussion which recalls the idea of 'being special'. Ask the children what they have remembered and understood about the concept

Learning objectives
● Think about how most of the people who are special to them love and care for them.
● Understand that they can make special people happy or sad.

Lesson organisation
Whole-class, teacher-led discussion with visual stimulus material; small group activities; plenary.

Being special

Vocabulary
special
valued
helping
caring
like
love
family
need
depend
near
far away

of being 'special' and about things that are valued. Look back at words and pictures which have been displayed to emphasise the ideas.

Show the children a poster of pictures of people behaving in a special way towards each other, such as a mother and a child together, a father or grandfather sharing an activity with a child, an adult picking up a child who has just fallen down and is upset.

Ask the children:

- Why might the grown-ups in the poster be described as special?

Try to sort out the children's answers into two categories: 'What do they *do* to make them special?' and 'What *kind* of people are they which makes them special?' Develop the ideas in the first category by asking the children what kinds of things grown-ups do to help children.

Share the photographs that the children have brought in and talk about other things adults do that make them special, for example taking a child to hospital or taking a child on holiday. The children may have brought in photographs of siblings, cousins or friends. Ask them to think of all the reasons why the people in their photographs are special. Give the children the opportunity to think of a word to describe the person in the photograph. Ask them:

- Is the person special for anyone else?
- Do you think the person realises that you think they are special?

Make a class list of the categories of people the children have described as special, for example *mother, friend...*

40 mins Development

Divide the children into groups to work on the following activities:

- Ask them to produce a small booklet about a special person of their choice, using the blank zigzag books you have provided. On the front cover they should draw a picture of the special person (or alternatively they could stick a photograph in its place) and add the words *My special person is _____ by _____*. They can use the following three pages to describe and draw what the person does and why this makes them special; what they share with them – activities they do together; what they feel about them – what it is about that person that makes them happy. Explain that the zigzag book should focus on what the person is like, perhaps using words such as *kind, gentle, caring*.

- Give out a selection of previously cut-out card body parts and ask the children to put them together to construct a jointed figure, using paper fastenings to connect together the head, body, arms and legs. Tell the children that the figure is now their special person and can be coloured, as appropriate. The figure can then be dressed in clothes made out of card, if the children so wish.

- Ask the children to describe their special person, writing key phrases on a separate piece of card, such as *My special person is special because they know about... My special person is good at... My special person is a very _____ sort of person.*

 Plenary
Give children from each group the opportunity to talk about what they have achieved. Ask some of the children in the first group to read their 'special person' books. Invite one or two of the children who made the jointed figures to talk about who the figures represent. Ask children in the third group to take turns to read out some of their completed sentences about their special people. Discuss the similarities and differences in their descriptions. Encourage the children to think about 'Is this what makes someone special?' Conclude by suggesting that the children set themselves a personal goal related to the idea of a 'special person': *I will try... for my special person.* Explain that they should ask themselves:

● What can I do to make my special person happy?
● What do I do that sometimes makes them sad?

Point out that it is often necessary to share a special person with someone else. For example, we have to share our parents with our brothers and sisters. How do the children feel about this? What have they had to do in the past to make this work?

Differentiation
Ask less able children to carry out the second group activity or, alternatively, if they are working on the first activity, make sure that an adult helper is available to discuss key words and phrases with them that would be appropriate for their zigzag books. Ask the more able children in the third group to develop their sentences into a short descriptive piece of writing.

Assessing learning outcomes
Can the children extend their understanding of the concept of 'special' to people rather than things? Do they appreciate that how people treat us affects how we feel about them? Are they gaining an understanding of the impact of people's behaviour on them and the impact of their behaviour on others?

ICT opportunities
Provide the children with a word-processed framework that allows them to put their 'special person' book on the computer (see 'Development'). The children's drawings could be scanned and placed on the relevant pages or clip art could be used.

Follow-up activity
Some of the children may have experienced the death of a special person or having to be parted from them for long periods of time. Read *Badger's Parting Gifts* by Susan Varley (Andersen Press) to the children. This is a story in which Badger's friends learn to come to terms with his death through their memories of him.

Why are people special?

What you need and preparation
Before the activity, arrange for a visiting speaker, such as a nurse, a firefighter or a police officer, to come to the school to talk to the children about an important aspect of their life within the community. Prepare the children for the visit by helping them to compile a list of questions that would be relevant, such as: *What does the person do? How do they help people? What do they have to be good at to do their job? Why do they think their job is important? Why are they special?*

Obtain some posters that show pictures of people doing jobs that help people, for example doctors, nurses, firefighters, police officers. Cut out pictures of well-known people from newspapers and magazines – these could be famous football players, film actors and pop stars – try to find pictures of a variety of people who are famous for different reasons. You will also need: cuttings taken from local newspapers about people in the community that show examples of their special achievements, such as acts of bravery, a disability that they have overcome, a special service to the community that they have made; board or flip chart; photocopiable pages 109 (with a selection of pictures of 'special people' for the children to choose from to stick on the box) and 110; glue; writing materials.

Learning objectives
● Recognise that they belong to various groups and communities, such as the school community.
● Understand that the skills and qualities of people within their immediate community and outside play a role in their own welfare and development.
● Realise that the individual's contribution is important for the whole community.
● Learn how to set simple goals.

Being special

Lesson organisation
Whole-class, teacher-led discussion with visual stimulus material; visit by member of the community to the school followed by brief question and answer session; individual or paired activity; plenary.

What to do

(25 mins) Introduction

Remind the children about their thoughts and ideas concerning who were their own special people. Let this lead into a discussion in which you introduce the idea of special and valued people outside their own families, friends and classroom. Who would be special and what sort of jobs would they do that make them special? Talk about people who help others, such as nurses and doctors, the school caretaker, refuse collectors, the school secretary. Encourage the children to tell you how they help us, for example refuse collectors prevent disease by removing rubbish, the school crossing patrol ensures our safety when crossing the road.

Ask the children:

● Who would you add to this list of special people?
● What is special and important about the person's job?
● What sort of skills and special qualities would you need for the job?

Now look at the posters of 'people who help us' and discuss other people who are special. Encourage the children to consider what life would be like if they were not there to help us. What sort of difficulties would arise?

Move on to looking at pictures of well-known people, such as famous footballers. Discuss their skills and qualities, and emphasise the difference between the two: skills are what people use to achieve a goal and qualities are aspects of their character that make them a 'special' person (and perhaps help them to achieve their goal). Give the children a simple example, such as a singer who has a very good voice (her skill) but who also shows kindness and consideration to others (her qualities); she demonstrates this by singing to raise money for charity or to entertain sick people.

Read short extracts from newspaper or magazine cuttings illustrating how people have contributed something of value to the local community through their actions, and record on the board key ideas that arise.

Now introduce the special visitor you have invited to the school and let them talk to the children about their job, skills and responsibilities or special contribution to the community. Give the children an opportunity to ask the person questions about the skills and qualities required in their job.

(25 mins) Development

Ask the children to work individually or in pairs to complete the 'Wanted' poster on photocopiable page 109. Provide them with a selection of pictures of 'special people' that they

Vocabulary
valued
skills
strengths
qualities
need
depend
support
brave
kind
patient
fair
considerate

can choose from to use in the box. Remind them that when they are answering the questions they will need to think of the skills and qualities that the person would need to fulfil the requirements of their job.

Plenary

20 mins Recap on the special skills and qualities the children have thought about during the activity. Would they regard some as more important than others? Do they see more examples of some than others? Which of the qualities have they experienced directly? Identify the various skills and qualities they would like to develop. Encourage them to set goals for themselves, recording them on a copy of photocopiable page 110.

Differentiation

Provide younger or less able children with a copy of photocopiable page 109 that has the statements completed, so that they can create a 'Wanted' poster by simply choosing a picture of a person whom they think matches the skills and qualities presented. Support children who are attempting to finish the statements themselves by guiding them in their choice of appropriate qualities.

More able children could use examples of famous people from history to illustrate their special contribution. Make sure that they have the resources (pictures and information) to complete photocopiable page 109 in this way.

Assessing learning outcomes

Do the children understand the distinction between skills and qualities? Are they able to appreciate the special contribution that individuals can make to their community? Can they make the link between what these people do and how it affects their own lives?

> **Follow-up activity**
> Ask the children to write a letter to the visitor, thanking them for their visit and explaining what they have learned from the discussion and the task they completed in the activity.

1 hour How am I special?

What you need and preparation

You will need: a small empty box covered in shiny paper for each group (inside the box there should be a mirror in the base); photocopiable page 111; board or flip chart; writing materials.

What to do

Introduction

25 mins Begin with a whole-class discussion in which you recap on the meaning of *special* and *valued*. Talk to the children about the previous activities they have done in which they wrote about their special things and special people. Encourage them to identify the important things they learned.

Direct the focus of the discussion to their classroom. Ask:
● What makes it different from other classrooms? (The physical difference – its size, shape, colour, equipment.)
● What do you like about the classroom?

> **Learning objectives**
> ● Recognise and value their own special qualities and appreciate that those of others are important.
> ● Respect the differences between people.

Being special

Lesson organisation
Whole-class, teacher-led discussion; small group activities with visual stimulus; plenary discussion.

Vocabulary
special
valued
important
loved
liked
skills
qualities
kind
fair
helpful
considerate
truthful

Talk about the children's perceptions of what goes on in their classroom, moving on to the idea that it is also the people that make it different and not necessarily its shape or size or what is in it. Ask the children why the people in it make it different from other classes in the school. Develop this beyond the idea of the children's ages and sizes to their different personalities – what makes classrooms different is that they contain children who have different knowledge, skills and qualities.

Record the children's key ideas about their class on the board, drawing a smiley face in the centre.

20 mins Development

Divide the children into groups, organised so that they are sitting at their tables. Place one shiny box with the lid closed on each table. Tell the children that there is something very special inside the box, but they must not touch it until it is their turn to look inside.

Invite the children to suggest what might be in the box. Then allow them to take turns to look in the box without speaking. The answer is a secret! (Supervise closely anyone likely to shout out.) The children will see their own reflection in the box.

When they have all looked in the box, share the secret – that they saw themselves – and ask the children what they felt. How are they special? Record their responses on the board, prompting them by talking about things they can do for themselves – their achievements. These can be skills or emotional/behavioural achievements. What are they getting better at? For example, *At the beginning of term I was on book 3 in reading, but now I'm on book 6.*

Distribute copies of photocopiable page 111 and ask the children to complete the starter sentences: *I am special because… I can… I know… I am…*

15 mins Plenary

Provide an opportunity for everyone to say something positive about someone else: _____ *is special because…* Reinforce the concept that everyone in the class is valued and has something to contribute. Focus on the positive and discuss how each member of the class can help every other person to make their group a special and happy one.

ICT opportunities
Ask the children to carry out the *I am special because…* exercise on the computer, adding a drawing using a scanned image or clip art.

Follow-up activities
● As a group activity, provide a sheet of paper with the name of a child in the group at the top. The sheet can then be folded over, as in a game of consequences, with the children taking it in turns to add their contributions about the person. Make sure the children understand that they are only allowed to write something that is positive.
● Repeat the activity but shift the focus, asking the children to write down suggestions about what makes a 'school' – a whole community of people – special.
● Read *Frog is Frog* by Max Velthuijs (Andersen Press) to the children, a story which celebrates the idea of being special because you are just yourself, or *Elmer* by David McKee (Red Fox).

Differentiation

In the discussion about the differences between the classrooms, help less able children to take part by using prompt cards on which you have written key words. For their work on the photocopiable sheet, provide them with statements which have already been completed and ask them to choose the ones that are appropriate, for example *I am good at making friends, I can keep a secret, I know lots about football, I am happy playing in the snow.*

Ask more able children to write about why they are special, using their own ideas and without reference to the framework of starter sentences on the photocopiable sheet.

Assessing learning outcomes

Are the children able to recognise and value their own qualities? Are they able to recognise and value the qualities of others? Can they extend the phrases *I am special because… I can… I know… I am…* into statements that make sense and show their understanding? Do they respect the differences between others and appreciate that people are special in different ways?

(1 hour) Which places are special to me?

What you need and preparation

Make a collection of pictures showing different 'special' places (for example, children in a playhouse or den; animals in their own particular habitat; a pet in its special basket). You will also need: a doll's house (optional); board or flip chart; cards with the words *I like to share my special place because…* or *I like to be alone in my special place because* written on them; paper; a blank Big Book; writing, colouring and drawing materials.

Before the activity, read extracts from a story describing a special or secret place, such as *The Secret Garden* by Frances Hodgson Burnett (Puffin). Alternatively, let the children watch the video of *The Secret Garden*.

What to do

(20 mins) Introduction

Begin by showing the children pictures of places that are special to different people or animals. Help the children to point out features that might make the places special. A tree house could be special, for example, because it is high up and far away from everyone; a sandy beach could be special because of its beauty and because it is a place where friends and family can be together and relax.

If you have read extracts from *The Secret Garden* (or another suitable book) before the activity, discuss aspects of the story in relation to it being a special place. Why was it special to different people – to Mary, her cousin, Colin, the robin, the gardener, Mary's guardian (Colin's father)? Talk about the different motives people had for wanting the garden to be a secret.

Move on to a more general discussion about how different places are special to different people. Make sure the children appreciate that it may not be obvious why a place is special; what is special to one person may not be special to someone else. Places can be special for a range of reasons, for example where someone was born, where they lived during childhood, where they first went on holiday, where they lived when they left home. Invite the children to talk about places that are special to them. Talk about places that are familiar to them, for example their bedroom, garden, a nearby park or play area. Develop their ideas by asking:

● How long has the place been special to you?

● Why is it special? What makes it special to you?

● Is it special to anyone else?

● Do you have a special place at home? Describe it.

● How do you feel if someone spoils your special place?

Give an example to help the children with the last question: in his bedroom a child builds a special tent from old sheets; it takes him a long time and a lot of effort to get it just right; he is really pleased with it when it is finished

Learning objectives
● Realise that different places in the environment are very important to different people.
● Understand that feelings are hurt when a person's place that is special to them is damaged in some way.

Lesson organisation
Teacher introduction; whole-class discussion; individual contributions towards a Big Book about special places.

Vocabulary
secret
shared
quiet
safe
alone
valued
important
personal
private
imaginary
pretend

and tells his family that no one is allowed to go in unless he gives them permission; however this makes his younger brother annoyed; he is too little to understand rules and regulations, and tears it all down (in five seconds flat!); how does the older child feel about losing his special tent? Point out that the older child was right to feel angry. However, if he had been willing to share his special place with his younger brother, it might not have been destroyed! Ask the children:

● How do you feel about sharing your special place?
● Do other people have special places that you share?

(30 mins) Development
Tell the children that they are going to make a book about their special places that everyone can read and share. Brainstorm descriptive vocabulary that they could include in their text and write key words on the board. Ask the children to draw their special place and then choose an appropriate card (either *I like to share my special place because…* or *I like to be alone in my special place because*) to complete.

(10 mins) Plenary
Invite the children to show their finished drawings and captions to the rest of the class, before they are collated and made into a Big Book

called 'Special places'. Ask what they have learned about different special places. Do they have things in common? What are the most significant differences?

Differentiation
Less able children may need helpful suggestions on what to include on their page of the book. Ask them to label their drawing of their special place with *I like to share* or *I like to be alone*.

More able children could create an imaginary special place or write a poem or a piece of extended descriptive writing about a special place. Music could be selected to accompany poems that the children read aloud.

Assessing learning outcomes
Do the children show an appreciation of what makes different places special for different reasons? Do they appreciate that other people have different special places? Are they able to express their feelings about sharing their special place or it being damaged?

ICT opportunities
Ask the children to key in their text about their special places at the computer. Each child's section of text can then be printed out and cut to size before being pasted into the Big Book on a page underneath their drawing. Encourage them to use different fonts, to give an individual feel to each page.

Follow-up activity
Ask the children to design a special place together, working as a whole class. Where would it be? What would it be like? What would it have in it? Write their suggestions on the board, as part of a class brainstorm, before finalised ideas are put down on paper.

Building friendships

The main focus of this unit is on helping children to think about how they can manage personal relationships effectively. It begins by encouraging children to consider the importance of past experiences and memories in forming their own image of themselves. Having a positive self-image is an important building block for creating and maintaining sound personal relationships.

The children are provided with opportunities to move from a self-centred view of themselves and their relationships to one where they begin to consider the effects of their behaviour and actions on other people. An understanding of the reciprocal nature of relationships will develop when children are around ten to eleven years old.

Children are offered a range of activities which help them to become aware of and explore their own networks and their place in them. They have opportunities to consider how these networks change and widen, sometimes bringing conflicts which need to be resolved. It is the process employed in the learning, the sharing, reflecting, comparing and assessing which is seen as helping children to develop this sensitivity towards other people's feelings.

The unit allows children to:
● reflect on the effect memory has in forming self-image
● recognise, name and deal with feelings in a positive way
● develop sensitivity to the needs and feelings of others
● reflect on the qualities and skills required in making and sustaining relationships
● recognise that they belong to various groups and communities such as families and schools
● recognise how their behaviour affects other people
● understand that family and friends should care for each other.

The structure of each activity within the unit allows children to develop skills for dealing with situations which involve building and maintaining friendships, and reflect on and assess experiences related to building and maintaining friendships.

Through a variety of stimuli you can introduce the focus of the session and use key questions to generate and develop discussion. The children can be given opportunities to share ideas and learning within a range of contexts and using a curriculum focus of literacy, art, music, and drama or role-play. Depending on the age and ability of the children, you can encourage them to consider the qualities, attitudes and values important in developing and maintaining relationships.

UNIT: Building friendships

Enquiry questions	Learning objectives	Teaching activities	Learning outcomes	Cross-curricular links
What do I remember?	● Learn that sharing their opinions on things that matter to them and explaining their views is valuable. ● Recognise that it is important to appreciate and understand how they have changed, and developed skills and knowledge.	Teacher-led discussion about memories and growing up. Paired and group activities: children talking about memories associated with particular objects, then focusing on more general memories.	Children: ● appreciate the importance of memories for their personal growth ● appreciate how much they have developed as individuals over the years ● recall both happy and sad memories	English: reading autobiographical stories – that is, stories that rely on memory.
How do I feel?	● Recognise different feelings and understand the importance of dealing with them in a positive way.	Analysis of pictures showing different emotions. Group or paired mimes, followed by discussion. Labelling pictures in groups. Categorising different types of music, and drawing pictures associated with different moods.	● recognise different emotions that people feel and understand the importance of trying to deal with them in a positive way ● express different emotions in a symbolic visual form	Music: understanding how music is used for particular purposes and to create different moods.
What makes a friend?	● Realise that friends have needs, and that they have responsibilities to meet them. ● Understand that their behaviour affects other people.	Group reading of a story about the nature of friendship, followed by discussion. Children describing their own friends, then putting names of friends on paper. Completion of A5 booklets about the qualities a friend needs to have.	● begin to appreciate what friends are and can be ● gain an understanding of the qualities necessary to establish and keep friendships	English: exploring friendships in stories.
What does it mean – to share?	● Understand what it means to share.	Children making up a story which shows that always refusing to share can be unhelpful and hurtful. Designing a badge or other award to recognise someone who has shown how to share with others.	● understand the meaning of sharing and the effect it can have on others if you don't share	English: examining different stories in which sharing is an important theme.
What do friends share?	● Understand that being able to share is an important quality in establishing friendships. ● Realise that what they like and dislike in friendships is important. ● Recognise the importance of playing and working co-operatively.	Teacher-led discussion which focuses on the importance of sharing in friendships. Group activities: completing starter sentences about the benefits and difficulties of sharing; home corner play; making patterns on paper; construction work; writing about the skills needed to work well in a group.	● appreciate the value of sharing for their own self-development ● cope with having to share resources to complete tasks ● express their feelings about both good and bad aspects of their work completed in a group	PE: working with others in teams, respecting other group members.
How do we keep friends?	● Realise that keeping friends is about learning about their likes and dislikes, about their strengths and weaknesses. ● Understand that keeping friends is about sharing their opinions on things that matter to them.	Looking at special objects that have been broken and relating this to broken friendships, in a whole-class discussion. Writing of group advice booklets on how to keep friends.	● move from the personal to a more general perspective in terms of keeping friendships ● are aware of the nature of broken friendships and the difficulty of always maintaining them ● are able to express their feelings about broken friendships and understand that when this happens it is normal to feel rejected.	Art and design: representing ideas and feelings about friendship.

(50 mins) What do I remember?

What you need and preparation

Ask the children to bring in from home any books, toys or other objects which stimulate memories of past experiences. These could include photographs of the children at a younger age or postcards. (Their parents and carers should be able to help them with this task, and it may be a good idea to send a letter to them explaining the activity.) For older children, you could obtain photographs of school events such as sports days and concerts in which they have been involved. Place a selection of the objects into a medium-sized cardboard box. You will also need: board or flip chart; writing materials.

What to do

(20 mins) Introduction

Ask the children if they can remember any special events or occasions from when they were younger. Introduce the idea that remembering things that have happened to us helps us to grow as people.

Show the children a large cardboard box labelled 'Memories'. Talk to them about the meaning of the words *memory* and *remember*. Can they remember something that happened to them last week? Last month? How far back can they remember? Ask them:

● If I say, 'I remember', what am I doing?
● If this box is full of memories, what does that mean? Can you see a memory?

Establish that memories can only be seen in the mind, and that certain objects or photographs can remind us of something that happened in the past. Take the objects out of the box, starting with two or three of the children's own, to stimulate interest. Invite the children concerned to talk about them. What memories do they have that are linked to the object? Record their ideas on the board and any useful vocabulary – words that are appropriate to recalling the past and how they feel.

Ask the children:
● Do you remember anything in particular about being a very young child?
● What do you remember about it?
● How have you changed as you have grown up?

> **Learning objectives**
> ● Learn that sharing their opinions on things that matter to them and explaining their views is valuable.
> ● Recognise that it is important to appreciate and understand how they have changed, and developed skills and knowledge.

> **Lesson organisation**
> Whole-class activity with teacher-led discussion; paired discussions; group activities; plenary.

> **Vocabulary**
> memory
> happy
> past
> recent
> later
> sad
> pleased
> proud
> small
> tiny
> old
> young

> memory
> happy
> sad
> old
> small

ICT opportunities
The children could key in a few
sentences about their memories at the
computer, and add a smiley or sad face,
depending on the nature of the memory.

Follow-up activity
Help the children to produce a shared
text on a large sheet of paper. This
could take the form of a rhyming poem
based on the format *When we were
three … When we were four…* with the
last line of the poem starting with the
words *Now we are…* Try to link their
ideas together, at the same time
incorporating a rhyming pattern.

20 mins Development
Organise the children into pairs within groups. Make sure that each
child has an object of their choice to talk about, and explain that they must
talk to their partner for one minute about a memory associated with the
object. The pairs should then swap over and repeat the exercise. Each child
whose turn it is to listen has to ask one question of their partner.

Next, provide each group with a large sheet of paper. Encourage them to
talk about anything that they remember about their life at that particular age
and to write it down. Encourage the children to use the vocabulary that you
have written on the board.

10 mins Plenary
Draw the groups back together to share their memories of when they
were younger. Talk about how memories can be happy or they can be sad.
Emphasise that there is nothing wrong with remembering something that is
sad and that sometimes it is only by acknowledging sad feelings that we are
able to move on and not think about them so much.

Differentiation

Less able children could draw a happy or sad face in the development activity and label it to
explain the memory rather than talking about a past experience and its link to an object. For the
writing element, an adult helper could be provided to move around the groups, helping the
children to record their ideas.

Assessing learning outcomes

Can the children appreciate the importance of memories for their personal growth? Do they
appreciate how much they have developed as individuals over the years? Can they recall both
happy and sad memories?

50 mins How do I feel?

What you need and preparation

Collect together some postcards of famous paintings which show people in different states of emotion, for example Picasso's *Weeping Woman* or *Dora Marr Seated*, or Ford Maddox Brown's *The Last of England*. Find some more pictures which would be suitable for display and also for children to look at in groups. These could include photographs of children displaying various emotions. Write out some labels which children can use to link to the pictures (*These are lonely people, these are angry people*, and so on). Prepare a set of cards, each with a feeling or emotion written on it, using photocopiable page 112 (one card for each child). You will also need: short pieces of music (extracts which are clearly of different moods); board or flip chart; writing, colouring and drawing materials.

> **Learning objective**
> Recognise different feelings and understand the importance of dealing with them in a positive way.

> **Lesson organisation**
> Teacher-led introduction; whole class activity; teacher-led discussion with visual and oral stimulus, leading to extended discussion/development; group and paired activities; plenary.

What to do

20 mins Introduction

Begin by showing the children pictures of people displaying different emotions. Discuss with them what they might be feeling and why. What can they see in the picture that reveals the emotion? *(That person looks happy because... those people are sad because...)*

Tell the children that they are going to play a game about feelings. Give each child a card and explain that it will tell them how they are feeling *(I am feeling lost, I am feeling confident,* and so on); they must not tell anyone else what their card says because they are going to mime the feeling for other children to guess what it is. Organise the children into groups or pairs and give them a few minutes to perform their mimes to each other.

Bring the groups back together and ask the children if they found it easy to guess what the emotion was. How do they feel when they see fear, anger or sadness, for example, in other people? Point out that emotions can be expressed by people's bodies as well as their faces.

Draw some symbols on the board that could express some of the feelings you have been talking about. Introduce the idea that it is possible to misread the true feelings of a person. What does it mean if someone is described as 'putting on a brave face'? Talk about how people learn to deal with their feelings in a positive way, as they get older. Demonstrate this by comparing their behaviour now when they cannot get something they want with how it might have been when they were two or three years old. A toddler hasn't yet learned to deal with his feelings in a positive way.

> **Vocabulary**
> happy
> sad
> angry
> worried
> lonely
> frightened
> laughing
> arguing
> shouting
> silent

20 mins Development

Provide each group of children with a selection of pictures or photographs that can be sorted into different categories of emotion. Encourage them to discuss the pictures before making a decision about the emotion being expressed. Explain that they should then label each

Building friendships

group of pictures with an appropriate card, for example *These are happy people*. When all the pictures have been categorised, provide time for each group to give feedback in a whole-class discussion.

Now play some short pieces of music to the children. Ask them to listen to the mood of the music each time and to find a group of pictures that 'matches' it. Label each group of pictures with a different letter. For example, they could say: *This is happy music – it makes me want to jump around the room. It fits the pictures in group A.*

Provide the children with strips of paper and replay the music. Ask them to draw shapes and symbols to express the feelings that come into their minds as they listen. Demonstrate this by making a few sample drawings on the board. Children may have many different ideas of their own. Encourage them to use colour to indicate the mood of the music.

10 **Plenary**
mins Invite the children to talk about what they heard in the music – the different feelings that were expressed by how fast it was, whether it was loud or quiet, or high or low. Look at examples of their symbols and shapes and the colours they have used. Explore how they vary depending on the piece of music.

Differentiation
Less able children may wish simply to use colours to express the feelings or mood of the music. Encourage them to listen carefully for any change of mood.

More able children could try to represent more complex emotions using symbols and colours and write an accompanying piece of explanation.

Assessing learning outcomes
Can the children recognise different emotions that people feel and understand the importance of trying to deal with them in a positive way? Can they express different emotions in a symbolic visual form?

ICT opportunities
Ask the children to make shapes or symbols to represent feelings, using clip art, and to give each picture an appropriate caption.

What makes a friend?

What you need and preparation
Select some books, stories, poems and pictures about friends and friendship, for example *Lucy's Quarrel* by Jennifer Northway (Scholastic: Hippo) or *Something Else* by Kathryn Cave and Chris Riddell (Puffin). You will also need: photocopiable page 113; blank A5 booklets; board or flip chart; writing, drawing and colouring materials.

What to do
30 **Introduction**
mins Tell the children that the focus of the activity is going to be on making and keeping friends. Remind them about previous activities in which they thought about special people and

Learning objectives
● Realise that friends have needs, and that they have responsibilities to meet them.
● Understand that their behaviour affects other people.

feelings. Ask them what they think is most important when making friends and why. Record their replies on the board.

Read a short story or poem about friends (see What you need and preparation). Ask the children to comment on what they have found out by listening to the story or poem. Try to bring out the importance of an awareness of treating people how you would like to be treated yourself. For example, at the beginning of the story of *Something Else* the main character is rejected even though he *did his best to be like the others.* When he has the chance to gain a special friend he nearly misses it because he momentarily rejects the new friend. He saves himself from further loneliness because he manages to realise what he is doing just in time – that is, treating people badly. Help the children to understand the power of individuals to break patterns of behaviour. The character Something Else sees that there is another way of behaving. Just because his 'friends' have rejected him, it doesn't mean that he then has to reject someone else, someone different, who wants to be friends with him.

Ask the children to close their eyes and think hard about a special friend, then write down four words to describe them. Select some children to describe their friends, using the words as prompts. Children can then name their friends, but be sensitive to new or shy children in the class. Invite some of the children to tell the others what it feels like to have a good friend. Stress that not all friends need to be school friends. A friend can live far away. A friend can be a member of one's family. Also, it is quite special to have an imaginary friend. Ask the children to talk about times when they have been a good friend to someone else.

Lesson organisation
Teacher-led discussion; whole-class story or poem; individual activities; plenary discussion.

Vocabulary
friendship
caring
sharing
thoughtful
kind
helpful
fair
unfair
true
selfish
unselfish
real

30 mins Development
Distribute copies of photocopiable page 113 and ask the children to complete the sheet by drawing a picture of themselves in the centre and then writing down names in each section to form their network of friends. Reassure them that they do not have to fill in each part, only the ones that apply to them. They could include pretend friends and animal friends, if they wish.

Provide the children with pre-prepared A5 booklets. Explain that on each page they must write a quality needed to be a friend. Suggest that they give the book the title *A friend needs to be...* or they could direct the focus onto themselves: *I would make a good friend because...* Alternatively, they could think of their own title.

ICT opportunities
The children could make a word-processed version of their network of friends (see photocopiable page 113). The class photograph could be taken with a digital camera, or scanned, and added to their work on 'My friends'.

10 mins **Plenary**
Select a few children to share their network of friends and to talk about the qualities a friend should have. If a child has an imaginary friend or a pet who is a best friend, reinforce how special this can be. Emphasise the importance of caring about our friends.

Take a photograph of the whole class together, including any classroom assistants. You could even include class pets. At a later date, display the photograph alongside completed copies of photocopiable page 113 and the A5 books. Give the display the heading *Our friends.*

Differentiation

Ask less able children to draw pictures of their friends rather than writing their names. They may also need help with 'grouping' their friends, through prompts and discussion.

More able children could extend their ideas about the qualities needed to be a friend by exploring *why* those qualities are important.

Assessing learning outcomes

Are the children beginning to appreciate what friends are and can be? Are they gaining an understanding of the qualities necessary to establish and keep friendships?

Follow-up activity
Invite the children to write a letter about themselves to send to a pen friend. They should describe what they like doing and what their interests are. They must remember that this is a friend whom they have never met, so they should make their letters as clear and interesting as they can. They could include why they think they would be a good friend: *I would be a good friend because…*

1 hour 20 mins What do friends share?

Learning objectives
● Understand that being able to share is an important quality in establishing friendships.
● Realise that what they like and dislike in friendships is important.
● Recognise the importance of playing and working co-operatively.

What you need and preparation

You will need: prepared starter sentences on cards (see Development); home corner or role-play area set up for 'pretend play' activities; construction sets or junk materials; large sheet of paper; drawing and colouring materials; photocopiable pages 114 (enlarged copy) and 115; board or flip chart.

What to do

20 mins **Introduction**
Begin with a whole-class discussion in which you recap on what makes a friend and the particular qualities of friends. Show the children the drawings of groups of children playing or working together on photocopiable page 114 and ask them to describe what is happening in the pictures. Do they think the children are friends? Encourage the children to give reasons for their answers. Point out the picture of the children skipping and ask the children what is different

about it. (It shows a child outside the group, watching.) Ask them why they think the child is not joining in.

Write the word *sharing* on the board. Ask the children what they think it means. Ask them how easy they find the idea of sharing *things*, then move on to the idea of sharing *friends*. What does *sharing* mean when we are with our friends? Develop the discussion to emphasise that sharing sometimes means sharing things with our friends and sometimes sharing our friends with others. It is good to share ideas and activities with our friends. Sometimes we share special secrets, and it can be hard to share our friends with others. Ask the children to recall a time when they did or did not manage to share a friend with someone else. How did they feel?

🕙 45 mins Development

Organise the children into groups, and give each group a prepared card which has an unfinished sentence written on it. For example:

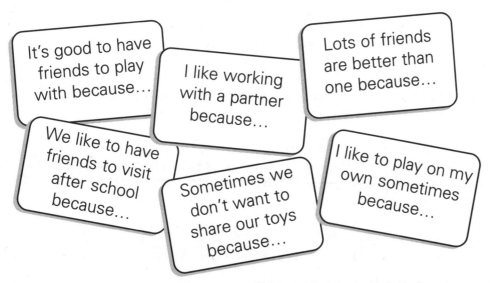

It's good to have friends to play with because…

I like working with a partner because…

Lots of friends are better than one because…

We like to have friends to visit after school because…

Sometimes we don't want to share our toys because…

I like to play on my own sometimes because…

Provide adult support for each group, if possible. Read out the start of the sentence with the children and then let them take it in turns to finish it off with an answer.

Give feedback on their responses and focus on the qualities of sharing. Encourage the children to say whether they think it is good to have time on one's own sometimes.

Now set each group to work on a different activity:

● In the home corner/role-play area, provide the children with a range of materials and resources to encourage creative play. Remind them of the importance of sharing these resources and playing together. Tell them that you are going to ask them to tell you the story of their 'pretend play' at the end of the session.

● Provide a group (no more than six children) with a large sheet of paper and felt-tipped pens. Explain that the task is to make a doodle or pattern on the paper. Four children start from the corners; two from the centre of the longest sides. They must work together to make a pattern or doodle, and it will be important for them to think carefully about the space they are using and how the pattern will work best. They will also need to agree on what colours to use.

● Ask a group to take part in a construction activity, providing them with the tools needed to complete the task. They must choose together what they are going to make from the construction kit (you could use junk materials as an alternative). Remind them of the importance of sharing and working together.

Lesson organisation
Whole-class, teacher-led discussion with visual stimulus; paired activities; small group activities; plenary discussion.

Vocabulary
sharing
co-operating
partner
pair
team
friend
couple
group
tolerance
respect

● Ask pairs to discuss the qualities they think a friend needs when working or playing in a large group. Explain that they should design a 'Wanted' poster (similar to the one they completed on photocopiable page 109), which could read: *Wanted: a friend to share in our games. This person needs to be… We need to be… to help you become part of our group.*

Plenary
15 mins Remind the children about the meaning of sharing. Ask them how they feel if someone refuses to share. Invite the group who played in the home corner to tell the rest of the class about their pretend play. Did they all manage to share the items they were playing with and was everyone given a chance to take part? Encourage the other three groups to talk to you in the same way about their sharing.

Provide each group with a copy of the self-assessment sheet on photocopiable page 115. Read through the statements and ask them to colour in the statements that they think match the way they have been working together. They must colour in one statement or more, even if not everyone agrees with the choices made.

Differentiation
Less able children should be encouraged to tackle the first and second activities – the home corner play and the 'Wanted' poster.

Assessing learning outcomes
Do the children appreciate the value of sharing for their own self-development? Do they cope with having to share resources to complete tasks? Are they able to express their feelings about both good and bad aspects of their work completed in a group?

How do we keep friends?
1 hour

What you need and preparation
Make a collection of 'special' things that have been broken. Some old chipped crockery and pots that you are not using anymore would be good examples. You will also need: prepared labels with statements that relate to how to keep friends (see Development); board or flip chart; writing materials.

What to do
20 mins **Introduction**
Introduce the children to some 'special' objects that have got broken. Ask them how they feel when they break things that are special to them or when they see special things broken. Write their responses on the board.

Move on from how they *feel* to what they *do* if something gets broken. Make a list on the board, perhaps separating the actions into positive and negative ones: *keep the bits; throw them away; tell someone else; keep worrying about it; get a new one; forget about it; say sorry; try to mend it,* and so on. If they wanted to mend the broken object, how could it be done – glue, string, tape, get a new part, ask an adult to take it to the shop?

Discuss what they can do when friendships get broken. What causes friendships to get broken. How does it feel? Explore with the children ways in which they can mend friendships and stay friends.

25 mins **Development**

Provide each table with some slips of paper on which you have written various strategies for keeping friends, for example *helping each other, sharing something, giving them something of yours* and so on. Encourage the children to think about the whole-class discussion. How can we keep our friends and mend broken friendships?

Give each child a single sheet of A5 coloured paper and explain that they are going to write a book called 'How to keep friends', within their groups. Explain that they should discuss their own ideas as well as looking at the text on the slips of paper before deciding how each individual is going to contribute to the group advice booklet.

15 mins **Plenary**

Discuss with the children what they have learned about keeping friends. What are the dos and don'ts of friendship? Get them to try to rank these in order of importance. Ask them to come up with some goals for the classroom and playground linked to making, sharing and keeping friends. Write the goals down on a large sheet of paper to make a poster and display it alongside their completed advice booklets.

Lesson organisation
Whole-class, teacher-led discussion; individual activity within groups; plenary session.

Vocabulary
partner
group
fair
unfair
right
wrong
good
bad
kind
unkind
sharing
mend

Differentiation

Organise the activity to match the needs, understanding and ability of the children. Less able children may need help with the booklet in the form of key words and headings. The contributions from individuals in the groups may also need to be specified.

Ask more able children to write their booklets individually, rather than in groups (they may also prefer to write their own title), and encourage them to consider the skills required in maintaining friendships. What is right and what is wrong, if you want to keep a friend? They could consider negative qualities, as well as positive qualities, exploring issues such as teasing, name-calling and other forms of bullying, and the impact of these forms of behaviour on friendships.

Assessing learning outcomes

Can the children move from the personal to a more general perspective in terms of keeping friendships? Are they aware of the nature of broken friendships and the difficulty of always maintaining them? Are they able to express their feelings about broken friendships and understand that when this happens it is normal to feel rejected?

ICT opportunities
The children could design the poster on making, sharing and keeping friends at the computer, using a variety of different coloured fonts and clip art.

Follow-up activity
Ask the children to a draw a picture about making and keeping friends and to take it home to show to their parents and carers.

Building healthy bodies

This chapter explores the all-important area of children's health and the development of behaviours and attitudes which will ensure that they grow up respecting their bodies (and minds) and adopting a healthy lifestyle. In order to achieve this goal, it is important that children understand and appreciate, from an early age, how their body works and also what they can do to ensure that it continues to 'work well' for them.

As children grow physically, their knowledge and awareness have to grow accordingly in order for them to make decisions about how they treat their body and to be clear about the implications and consequences of those decisions. At the same time, they will come to a growing recognition of the pressures on them in terms of 'healthy living'. Sometimes these pressures may be 'healthy' pressures – encouragement to take exercise, advice on what to eat and not to eat, suggestions on how to relax and cope with stress. At other times, as they grow older, they may be of a different nature and less beneficial, such as the pressure to eat the same type of food that their peer group is eating (food which is not necessarily healthy!), to stay up too late watching television and playing computer games, to experiment with smoking and alcohol (and other drugs) – all activities which put strain on their bodies and put them at risk. They will also begin to realise that these pressures come from a wide variety of contexts, some of which are familiar – friends, acquaintances, maybe even family – and some of which are less familiar, but nevertheless as close to them in terms of the power of their influence – the media, the music scene, any culture with which they are beginning to identify.

There are a number of balances which have to be achieved in this particular area of children's development, none of which are easy! There is the balance between, on the one hand, being too negative and 'playing up' the dangers or worrying elements to the exclusion of anything else and, on the other hand, having a sort of blind faith in which positive ideas and attitudes conducive to healthy living are expected to surface of their own accord without adult intervention. Another balance that needs to be worked out is between not telling children what to do at all times and being prescriptive, even dogmatic, and not allowing them to reach decisions and make up their own minds before they are mature enough to do so. Finally, a balance needs to be sought between differing values and opinions from different sources; personal belief systems that conflict with each other. It may be school versus home, or the home versus the community – it is often a conflict which involves the child's parents/carers (and teachers) and the child's peer group. As children mature beyond primary school, it is their peer group which is likely to have the greatest effect on their behaviour and how they look after their bodies.

My body

This unit provides activities which are designed to help children's growing understanding and appreciation of how their body works and how, as they grow, they will demand more and more of their body, in terms of its strength, flexibility, health and fitness. They will also be encouraged to begin to think about how they have a responsibility to look after and care for their bodies and make sensible choices. Children of this age group may have limited powers and opportunities for decision-making but they need to be provided with knowledge that will prepare them for the gradual process of acquiring them. This is vitally important as, if they do not make the right choices, it will affect their lives and probably those of their immediate family and friends.

This unit will develop children's understanding of the different parts of their bodies and how those parts interact with each other; how their bodies make them both similar and different from others; how their bodies change as they get older; how growing up brings responsibility and independence. There will inevitably be sensitive areas for discussion – some children will be particularly self-conscious of their bodies and anxious about what will happen to them as they grow up, and other children may take the opportunity to exploit those children by playing on their fears and misgivings. It is important to ensure that all children are given the chance to express their opinions freely, but in an environment – that is, the classroom – in which the threat of criticism and unkind remarks from others has been removed.

UNIT: My body

Enquiry questions	Learning objectives	Teaching activities	Learning outcomes	Cross-curricular links
What can my body do?	• Learn the names of the main parts of the body. • Recognise how different parts of our body make us similar and different from others.	Introductory song and demonstration of how different parts of the body move. Identification of simple names of different parts of the body. Whole-class discussion of differences in people's physical appearance. Individual activity: children drawing a simplified diagram of their bodies and adding descriptive phrases about their appearance.	Children: • identify and name the main parts of the body • appreciate the differences and similarities between themselves and others • talk about differences sympathetically and with understanding of others' feelings	Science: recognising similarities between themselves and others; recognising the main external parts of the body.
How does my body work?	• Understand that different parts of the body have specific functions. • Realise that different parts of the body work together.	Teacher-led discussion about the functions of different parts of the body. Group activities: matching statements to correct body parts; role-play in which children imagine that they are different parts of the body.	• describe what each part of the body does • describe how different parts of the body work together • put themselves in the role of a part of their body	English: role-play, using their imagination as well as factual knowledge about the human body and its different parts.
How am I growing and changing?	• Recognise that as they grow up they will change in different ways. • Learn that as they grow up they will become increasingly independent.	Whole-class discussion in which key stages in children's growth are recorded. Visit by a mother and baby. Analysis of what it means to be more grown-up. Sorting pictures of people of different ages and writing key statements. Group activities focusing on different stages of growth.	• talk about things they did when they were younger • compare 'then' and 'now' • identify different stages of growth by assessing a person's skills • appreciate the perspective of their parents and carers	Science: grouping living things according to observable similarities and differences; understanding how humans grow.
How do I feel about...?	• Recognise that the process of growing from young to old involves feelings and emotions. • Realise that other people have needs, and that they have responsibilities to meet them. • Understand that people's needs and responsibilities change as they grow older.	Group story or poem followed by discussion about feelings to do with growing up and learning to take on more responsibility. Individual activity: children identify responsibilities that they are being given as they become older.	• appreciate the relationship between growing up, being responsible, making choices and developing feelings • understand the idea of emotional development as well as physical development	English: writing a story or a poem about the benefits and 'hazards' of growing up.
What if my body couldn't...?	• Learn to respect the differences between people. • Understand that being unable to do certain things can create both positive and negative feelings. • Realise that some people develop personal strengths which compensate for their inability to carry out physical tasks.	Teacher-led discussion about disabilities. Whole-class or group activity in which potential difficulties brought about by a situation where people's disabilities have not been taken into account are pinpointed, with practical solutions being discussed.	• appreciate the challenges that disabled people face • identify with their needs and understand that they develop skills to enable them to manage their lives successfully.	Design and technology: evaluating suitability for practical use and safety of a design, talking about ideas and discussing improvements that can be made.

 What can my body do?

What you need and preparation
Gather together a selection of 'body' books and posters which show pictures of different parts of the body and which focus on how the body grows and changes. It would also be useful to be able to show similarities and differences between different individuals. You will also need: a life-size drawing of the outline of a child's body for display; prepared labels of body part names; board or flip chart; paper; writing, drawing and colouring materials.

What to do
Introduction
Begin by singing 'Heads, shoulders, knees and toes' with the children, or any other 'body' songs that they know. Then ask three or four children to stand at the front of the class and to move different parts of their bodies in as many ways as they can. They could begin by making simple movements with their arms and legs. Try to get each child to demonstrate a different movement.

Invite the class to find words and phrases to describe what the children at the front are doing and how they are doing it. Encourage them to name the parts of the body that are being used. Give them some help, if necessary, for example *they are waving their hands and bending their wrists*. Ask them to name any other parts of the body that they can see (some children may name internal organs, which can also be acknowledged, but remind them that they cannot be seen!).

Look at the books and posters together, and draw the children's attention to the drawn life-size body outline on display. Invite them to attach the prepared labels to the correct body parts.

Now select children who have some similarities and differences in their appearances, for example height; colour and length of hair; colour of eyes. Encourage the class to describe the children (be sensitive towards children's feelings about their shape and size), for example *Stephanie is tall – she has long legs; Robert has wide shoulders; Ashi's hair is long, straight and dark.* Develop the idea that although we all have the same body parts, we look different from each other. That is what makes us all individual and special. Encourage language development: *bigger, smaller, taller, shorter, smallest* and so on. Talk about identical twins and how difficult it is to tell them apart. Do they have any ideas about how a person might distinguish between twins?

Learning objectives
● Learn the names of the main parts of the body.
● Recognise how different parts of our body make us similar and different from others.

Lesson organisation
Song and whole-class, teacher-led discussion; individual activity; plenary.

Vocabulary
head
shoulders
arms
legs
neck
elbow
wrist
knees
hair
eyes
nose
ears

CHAPTER 2

My body

ICT opportunities
The children could use a software program to position and label parts of the body.

Follow-up activities
● Play the game 'Simon says' to test the children's knowledge of names of different parts of the body. One person stands at the front of the class and gives directions to the other players. They must only follow the instruction if it begins with the words *Simon says* (for example, *Simon says touch your toes*). If it is just a straightforward command without the words *Simon says* (for example, *Stretch your arms*) then they must not follow it; if they do they are out of the game. Continue until there is only one player left, who is the winner.
● Ask some children to attempt a photofit drawing of another child using a written description of what they look like.
● As part of an art and design activity, let the children take their own fingerprints. The fingerprints can then be enlarged on the photocopier and compared as part of a study on people's differences.
● Take photographs of individual members of the class and put them together with pictures of other children from different countries. Help the children to appreciate people's similarities and differences around the world.

20 mins **Development**
Provide the children with a sheet of paper which has a heading *My special body*. Ask the children to draw themselves and label the parts of the body appropriately. Tell them that they should include main parts of the body and joints (for example, wrists, elbows, ankles). They could also include details such as their hair colour and height to give a short description of themselves, for example *This is my special body. I have a big smile. My eyes are... I am not as tall as...*

10 mins **Plenary**
Select several children to show their drawings and descriptions of themselves to the rest of the class. Are they happy with the final result? How accurate do they think they have made them? Reinforce the fact that the children have individual characteristics that make them different from one another.

Differentiation
When they are working on 'My special body', less able children may need visual clues in the form of labelled pictures in order to draw an accurate annotated diagram of their bodies. Encourage more able children to give an extended description of themselves. They could give more information about the different parts of their body, using children's encyclopedias for reference.

Assessing learning outcomes
Are the children able to identify and name the main parts of the body? Are they able to appreciate the differences and similarities between themselves and others? Are they able to talk about differences sympathetically and with understanding of others' feelings?

1 hour 5 mins How does my body work?

Learning objectives
● Understand that different parts of the body have specific functions.
● Realise that different parts of the body work together.

What you need and preparation
You will need: a selection of body books and pictures; board or flip chart; photocopiable page 116; writing materials.

What to do
15 mins **Introduction**
Discuss with the children the function of different parts of the body and the concept of co-operation. We need our mouths to take in food. We need our teeth to help us to chew. We need our eyes and ears to see and hear what is going on. Ask them to think of things they do which require different parts of the body working together, for example crossing a road or playing a game. Ask the children to help you make a list on the board of the parts of the body that work together.

Show the children a copy of the photocopiable sheet that they will be working on. Discuss some of the examples given and encourage them to make suggestions of their own, for example

Our back helps us to stand up straight. We can use our hands to make signs. Our feet help us to walk.

(35 mins) Development

Organise the children into small groups, and give out copies of photocopiable page 116. Ask the children to match each statement to the correct part of the body.

Move on to a role-play exercise. Give each child a part of the body to 'role-play'. Encourage them to introduce themselves and explain what their part of the body does, for example *I'm legs and I help you to walk.*

(15 mins) Plenary

Encourage the children to share what they have learned in the activity by inviting them to devise a short statement that explains the simple function of each part of the body: *My legs help me to... My eyes help me to...* and so on. Ask them to try to think of statements which relate to different parts of the body working together, for example *My brain helps my legs to walk.*

Differentiation

Help less able children with the role-play activity by first talking with them about what they will say and how they will incorporate their words into the action. More able children could role-play different parts of the body simultaneously.

When the children are completing the photocopiable sheet, encourage those of higher ability to create some extra statements for corresponding parts of the body. These can be written on the back of the sheet.

Assessing learning outcomes

Are the children able to describe what each part of the body does? Can they describe how different parts of the body work together? Can they put themselves in the role of a part of their body?

Lesson organisation
Teacher-led, whole-class discussion; small group activities; plenary.

Vocabulary
brain
skeleton
stomach
arms
energy
legs
elbow
wrist
back
neck
shoulders

Follow-up activity
It may be possible for someone who has a disability to visit the school and talk about how they cope with everyday situations.

CHAPTER 2

My body

1 hour 5 mins

How am I growing and changing?

Learning objectives
● Recognise that as they grow up they will change in different ways.
● Learn that as they grow up they will become increasingly independent.

Lesson organisation
Whole-class, teacher-led discussion; group activities; plenary.

Vocabulary
growing
changing
tall
small
big
high
young
older
cry
walk
talk
climb

What you need and preparation

Before the activity, invite the children to bring in pictures of themselves when they were babies. Prepare a selection of pictures to complement these of people of all ages (see Development). Arrange a visit to the class by a mother and baby, if you wish to include this part of the activity. (Prior to the visit, help the children to think of questions they would like to ask the baby's mother.) You will also need: photocopiable page 117; board or flip chart; large sheets of paper; writing, drawing and colouring materials.

What to do

Introduction

20 mins Talk with the children about what they recall about being a very young child. It is unlikely that they will remember anything before the age of three but do they know, from what their parents and carers have told them, what they could do as a baby? Have they seen photographs of themselves when they were babies. What are the different stages of babyhood? When did they learn to walk, talk, sit up, and so on? Encourage the children to talk about younger brothers or sisters or other babies they know. What have they seen them do? Record key stages in their growth on a class chart.

If possible, ask a mother and baby to come into the school to talk to the children. During the visit, encourage the children to make comparisons between themselves and the baby, and make sure that at the end they ask the questions that they have prepared.

After the talk, show the children pictures of babies, toddlers, young school children and older children. Look at the children's own pictures of when they were babies. Ask them:
● How do you know you have grown?
● Can you describe how you have changed?
● What do you think you can do now that you couldn't do when you were much younger?
Introduce the word *independent* and ask the children to give you definitions for the word,

for example 'doing things on your own'. How have they become more independent? Encourage them to think of the positive things about being more independent. What do they think their parents think about them 'growing up'? Record key vocabulary, relating to developing skills, on the board.

35 mins Development

Provide the children with a collection of pictures cut out from magazines. The pictures, each one mounted on a large sheet of paper, should include babies, toddlers, children, teenagers and adults. Invite the children to sort them into different stages of growth and development. Explain that they must then add a caption, using the key words on the board, for example:

These babies can…
These toddlers can…
These children are bigger and older and can…

Divide the class into three groups and provide each group with a large sheet of paper. Set each group to work on one of the following activities, asking them to:

● Discuss what they could do when they were a baby, then describe this stage of their development, for example *When I was a baby I could cry, crawl… When I was a baby I couldn't walk about, talk…*

● Finish the starter sentence *I know I am growing because…*, recording their thoughts on the paper, for example *…I can't fit in my baby chair …I needed a new bed …my dress is too short …I had to have a new coat.* Encourage the children to think about different parts of their body that have grown, for example *My hands – I needed new gloves. My legs – my trousers don't fit. My feet – I needed new pumps. My head – my hairband is too tight. My hair – I keep having to have it cut. My teeth – some of them are falling out and new ones are growing.*

● Think about things that they can now do because they have grown, writing about them using the format *Now I am older, I can…* How have they become more independent? For example, they might say *Now that I am older, I can reach the biscuit tin …feed myself …get myself dressed …tie my own shoelaces …answer the telephone …climb the wall bars …go to school …write about what I can do.*

In each activity, the children could draw pictures to illustrate their text.

10 mins Plenary

Discuss the work that the children have completed in the group activities. Start by drawing their attention to the pictures and captions which show people at varying stages of growth. Focus on the differences between the stages such as body shape, physical characteristics, nature of skills and level of independence.

Invite the children to share their experiences of growing up, and discuss the idea of increasing responsibility in their lives – in school and at home. Encourage them to ask their parents and carers to give them more details about how they have grown and developed since babyhood.

My body

Follow-up activities
• Invite the mother and baby back to the school in a year's time. The children will be fascinated by how much growth has taken place! Ask the mother to talk about the changes that have occurred in the baby's height, weight, feeding and so on.
• Encourage the children to keep a diary entitled 'Growing up' in which they record the milestones in their development and add photographs or drawings of themselves.

Differentiation

Provide adult support for less able children in the first group activity, to help them write the captions for the pictures showing differing stages of development. They could also complete the writing frame on photocopiable page 117. Ask more able children to carry out the last group activity in which the focus is on their independence, as it will give them more opportunities to extend their ideas based on their understanding and experience.

Assessing learning outcomes

Are the children able to talk about things they did when they were younger? Are they able to compare 'then' and 'now'? Can they identify different stages of growth by assessing a person's skills? Are they able to appreciate the perspective of their parents and carers?

①hour How do I feel about…?

Learning objectives
• Recognise that the process of growing from young to old involves feelings and emotions.
• Realise that other people have needs, and that they have responsibilities to meet them.
• Understand that people's needs and responsibilities change as they grow older.

Lesson organisation
Story or poem and teacher-led discussion; individual activities; plenary.

What you need and preparation

Make a collection of pictures of people of all ages with different facial expressions – happy, sad, angry, frustrated, worried, and so on. You will also need: a simple story or poem about growing up, for example *I Want To Be* by Tony Ross (Andersen Press); photocopiable page 118; writing materials.

What to do

30 mins Introduction
Begin the activity with a story or a poem about growing up (see above). Talk to the children about how we grow not only physically but mentally. Our bodies grow, but we also change as people – our personalities, our feelings and emotions 'grow'. Talk to the children about growing up at home; how perhaps they share in activities with parents and carers, and gradually find that they are being given small amounts of responsibility, helping them to develop as an individual. Are there any things they are starting to do that worry their parents and carers? Are they allowed to cross the road on their own; go out on their bike; go to the local shop? Explain to the children that these activities are all about being grown-up enough to

My body

be responsible in a way that uses their mind as well as their body.

Show the children the pictures of different people and ask them to identify the feelings shown on their faces. Ask the children to use different facial expressions on their own faces to mirror the emotions they see. Move on to asking them to express different feelings with their whole body. Explain that how they *feel* is just as important as what they *do* as they grow up. Their bodies grow and change, helping them to find new skills, but their minds also need to develop. Discuss the idea of how growing up means becoming more aware of their feelings –

Vocabulary
growing
independent
changing
skills
feelings
confident
responsible
caring
sharing

for family, friends, pets. They are sad if they are ill; they are happy and excited if something nice happens to them; they worry if they're not happy.

Development

20 mins Give out copies of photocopiable page 118 and ask the children to complete the sentences to describe some of their responsibilities at home, at school and when they are with their friends. Explain that they must think of skills that they have developed, now that they are growing up. For example, at home they may be expected to tidy up their toys when they have finished playing with them (they may not be expected to cook meals); at school they may be expected to keep quiet when the teacher is talking (they may not be expected to answer telephone calls); their friends may expect them to play with them at lunchtime (they may not expect them to cut their hair for them).

ICT opportunities
Ask the children to write their story or poem about growing up at the computer (see 'Follow-up activities') and illustrate it using clip art.

Plenary

10 mins Allow the children to share what they have discussed and written. How do they feel about being given a responsibility at home or at school? Talk about what they think are their most important responsibilities.

Differentiation

Provide less able children with a selection of statements that they can choose from to complete the photocopiable sheet. Ask more able children to think of responsibilities they may have in the future. What sort of choices will they need to make? Ask them to write down their ideas on the back of the photocopiable sheet.

Assessing learning outcomes

Are the children able to appreciate the relationship between growing up, being responsible, making choices and developing feelings? Do they understand the idea of emotional development as well as physical development?

Follow-up activities
● Ask the children to write a story or a poem about growing up. How could they describe the process? What are their new responsibilities? What would other people notice about how they have changed?
● Arrange a visit from older children in the school (Years 4 and 5) to your class to talk about their experiences of 'growing up'. What have they learned that they did not know when they first started school? Are they now given responsibility to make their own decisions about some things?
● Focusing on emotions, the children could write about a subject which makes them have strong feelings, for example cruelty to animals.

My body

① What if my body couldn't…?
(hour)

Learning objectives
● Learn to respect the differences between people.
● Understand that being unable to do certain things can create both positive and negative feelings.
● Realise that some people develop personal strengths which compensate for their inability to carry out physical tasks.

Lesson organisation
Teacher-led discussion; whole-class or group activity; plenary.

Vocabulary
disability
strengths
capable
support
help
positive
caring

Follow-up activity
Invite someone who has a disability to talk to the children about their daily life.

What you need and preparation
You will need: photocopiable page 119; highlighter pens.

What to do

⑳ Introduction
mins This activity explores the sensitive area of disability and it is intended to help all children share in the insights and feelings associated with disability. If there are any children in your class who have disabilities, make sure that you involve them in a way that is comfortable to them.

Introduce the subject by saying that everyone of us in some way or other is not able to do things that others can – maybe some people cannot swim, sing in tune, play the piano, and so on. Some people, however, have to cope with other disabilities – perhaps they are not able to see, to walk, to hear. They are, in many cases, able to lead normal lives. Discuss with the children how this is made possible, for instance someone who cannot walk can use a wheelchair; someone who cannot see can have a special dog to guide them; someone who cannot hear can learn to lip-read and to use sign language. Some of the children may know of someone with a disability and can explain in more detail about what helps them in their daily lives.

Talk to the children about the problems that a disabled person may experience – what things would it be difficult for them to do that other people find easy? For example, a person who has a wheelchair cannot go up steps. Some of the children may have seen people with disabilities managing for themselves in certain situations. Emphasise that these people learn new and very crucial skills in order to live their lives in the same way as people who do not have their disabilities.

㉕ Development
mins Provide the children with copies of photocopiable page 119 and ask them to highlight problem areas for a disabled person (the steps, for example). Encourage them to think carefully about why the things they have identified would cause difficulties. What could be done?

⑮ Plenary
mins Encourage the children to give feedback on their completed photocopiable sheets. Talk to them about the achievements of people with disabilities, for example the paralympics.

Assessing learning outcomes
Are the children able to appreciate the challenges that disabled people face? Are they able to identify with their needs and understand that they develop skills to enable them to manage their lives successfully?

What I can do for my body

Having introduced the children in the first unit to the process of growing up and their developing physical and emotional skills, together with the exploration of ideas such as responsibility and respect, the second unit continues this theme, focusing on the particular area of developing a healthy lifestyle.

With some of the current health warnings relating to young children's eating habits and lack of adequate exercise, the issues tackled in this unit are particularly crucial to children's health as well as social development. In many respects the relationship between these two areas is a fundamental one, in that for some children the general state of their health and fitness directly relates to their social well-being and sense of self-esteem.

Making sensible and balanced choices coupled with a sense of responsibility is also a central feature of this unit. Children are influenced by the behaviour of others in their decision-making on lifestyle even at this age, whether it be friends or parents or by what they see advertised in the media. Equally, it is important for them to realise how they themselves can influence the behaviour of others, by persuading friends, or even by making demands of parents and carers, to follow their example.

This unit will develop children's understanding of:
- health-related matters affecting their own lives and those of others
- the influence of parents, friends and the media on people's lifestyles
- the value of balance in terms of eating and exercise.

It will also help them to explore attitudes and values related to a positive self-image, to focus on concepts of respect and worth, both for themselves and others, and to think about opinions on 'What is a healthy lifestyle?' which match or differ from their own.

There will inevitably be a possibility of a conflict of values emerging in some of the discussions that arise in the activities. In particular, the issue of healthy living – a balanced diet and sensible exercise – is often in conflict with the pace and nature of modern family life. Some children may have parents or carers whose lifestyles are far from healthy, and sensitivity towards these children, as far as these issues are concerned, will be required during discussions.

UNIT: What I can do for my body

Enquiry questions	Learning objectives	Teaching activities	Learning outcomes	Cross-curricular links
What does my body need?	• Recognise that they can make simple choices that may improve their health and well-being.	Teacher-led discussion about healthy and unhealthy lifestyles. Group activities: painting pictures of healthy and unhealthy people; writing possible reasons for people feeling well or unwell; deciding on choices healthy people may make about their lifestyles.	Children: • provide possible reasons for people feeling healthy or unhealthy • appreciate that people can make choices to improve their health and well-being	Science: understanding that taking exercise and living sensibly can help people to stay well.
Is it good for me?	• Learn how to make simple choices that improve their health and well-being. • Understand that choosing certain foods can help us to be more healthy.	Whole-class discussion about foods. Group activities: categorising different foods into 'healthy' and 'unhealthy'; stating food preferences. Further discussion followed by children writing statements about food choices they have made themselves.	• recognise healthy food, distinguishing it from food that is less healthy • are aware of the necessity to make the right choices about food, so that they are eating food that is good for them • understand that what other people choose to eat and what they see in advertising can influence their choices	Science: knowing that humans need food and water to stay alive; understanding that eating the right types and amounts of food help humans to keep healthy.
How can I learn about healthy food?	• Seek out information about healthy food and the way it is displayed in shops.	Children visiting a supermarket to look for healthy foods and recording any examples of food that is being promoted as a 'healthy eating' product.	• develop an awareness of the importance of learning about how food on sale is presented	Art and design: looking at similar products to study differences in the packaging.
How can I look after myself?	• Understand that keeping their bodies clean helps to protect them from infection. • Recognise that maintaining personal hygiene can improve their confidence and self-esteem.	Labelling of a picture by the teacher in consultation with the children during a discussion about skin hygiene and skincare. Sorting of products into two boxes: ones which are good for their bodies and ones which should be removed. Individual activity: assessing pictures and writing captions.	• understand that there are reasons for applying some substances to our bodies and removing others • appreciate that looking after their bodies can improve both their health and their self-esteem	Design and technology: investigating and evaluating a range of familiar products.
Have you ever been ill?	• Understand that some illnesses can be caught, but can often be controlled by taking the necessary action. • Realise that medicines can make them better, but can be harmful if they are not used properly.	Teacher-led discussion about coping with being ill, with recording of children's responses in preparation for making class book. Group activity: writing reasons for feeling better and drawing accompanying pictures on pages to be collated into a second class book.	• understand that there are many common illnesses that are spread by contact with other people • are aware that there are ways of reducing the spread of these illnesses • understand that medicines can help to make them better, but that medicines can be dangerous if they are not used properly.	Science: understanding the role of medicines when people are ill.

What does my body need?

What you need and preparation
You will need: board or flip chart; large sheets of paper; large blank speech bubbles (one speech bubble for each child); photocopiable pages 120 and 121; scissors; glue; writing, drawing and art/colouring materials.

What to do

Introduction
15 mins
Begin by asking the children how they feel today. Record their responses on the board. Then tell them how you are feeling and why. Explain that everyone is feeling well because they are healthy, but sometimes people can become ill through no fault of their own – they contract an illness. However, even when people are feeling well, there is a great deal that they can do to keep themselves fit and healthy. It is about making the right choices, and in order to make the right choices we need to have the correct information.

Write two headings on the board: *Healthy* and *Not so healthy*. Ask the children to offer ideas that could go into each category, for example *eat lots of fresh fruit and vegetables; play in the fresh air* is 'healthy' and *stay up late watching television; eat lots of sweet things* is 'not so healthy'.

Development
50 mins
Divide the children into two groups and give a large sheet of paper to each child. Explain that one group must paint or draw a picture of what they think a healthy person looks like, and the other group must paint or draw a picture of what they think a person who is not so healthy looks like. (Alternatively, you could ask each child to draw one picture for each category.) Tell the children that they could show whether people are 'healthy' or 'unhealthy' by what they are doing as well as what they look like.

Learning objective
Recognise that they can make simple choices that may improve their health and well-being.

Lesson organisation
Teacher-led discussion with visual stimulus; individual and group activities; plenary session.

Vocabulary
healthy
poorly
exercise
sleeping
resting
eating
feeling well/unwell
energetic
tired

**What I can do
for my body**

ICT opportunities
Invite the children to key in their text for their drawings at the computer. It can then be printed out, cut to size and pasted onto the speech bubbles. Encourage the children to use a variety of different fonts, to emphasise the differences in how their drawn figures are 'feeling'.

Follow-up activities
• Invite a doctor, nurse or fitness expert to come to the school to talk to the children about staying healthy.
• Ask the children to design a humorous cartoon poster about the dangers of being unhealthy.
• Provide the children with blank zigzag books and ask them to make a book of dos and don'ts regarding healthy living, for example *do eat breakfast every morning; don't always travel by car.* (They could refer to photocopiable page 120 for ideas.) Suggest that they write and draw a 'do' or a 'don't' on alternate pages and give their books the title 'Let's be healthy'.

Give out some large blank speech bubbles, one for each picture drawn by the children, and ask them to write in the speech bubble a possible reason for the person they have drawn being healthy (if they are in the first group) or being not so healthy (if they are in the second group). For example, they could write *I feel great – I went to bed early* or *I feel tired – I went to bed really late.* Or *I feel fit because I went for a long walk in the fresh air* or *I don't feel well because I ate too much chocolate.* Ask the children to paste their completed speech bubble onto their picture.

Now provide the children with copies of photocopiable pages 120 and 121. Ask them to cut out the phrases from the first sheet and choose a maximum of four different statements to place in each column on the second sheet under *Always*, *Sometimes* or *Never*. Remind the children that in this activity they are showing that people can make choices about how healthy their lives are.

Plenary
15 mins Invite a selection of children to talk to the rest of the class about their finished pictures. What did they write in their speech bubbles? How did the healthy people feel and how did this contrast with how the unhealthy people felt?

Ask the children to refer to their completed copies of photocopiable page 121 to help you to compile a class chart on the board, using the same format. What choices did they make? Fill in each column, writing down the phrases from photocopiable page 120 and encouraging the children to offer you further ideas. Discuss the category *sometimes* (for example, *sometimes watch too much TV; sometimes eat lots of sweets; sometimes stay up late*). Tell the children that *sometimes* may be fine, but that they must not forget that there is the danger of it easily becoming *always*!

Differentiation
Less able children may need an adult helper to scribe what they wish to say in the speech bubble for their drawing. More able children could take responsibility for the content of their charts on photocopiable page 121 themselves, without using the phrases on the first sheet.

Assessing learning outcomes
Are the children able to provide possible reasons for people feeling healthy or unhealthy? Are they able to appreciate that people can make choices to improve their health and well-being?

 ## Is it good for me?

What you need and preparation
Cut out some pictures from magazines of a range of different foods, both healthy and unhealthy – cereals, meats, fruit, vegetables, dairy produce, sweets and cakes, ready meals and so on. You will also need: board or flip chart; paper; labels made from card (each showing a smiley face or a sad face); blank self-adhesive labels; sheets of card; glue; writing, drawing and colouring materials.

What to do

20 mins **Introduction**
Discuss with the children the fact that eating is one of the things we do every day. We need food to stay alive and to help us to develop stronger bodies. Ask them, 'Why do we eat?' There may be a variety of responses, such as *because I am hungry; because it is dinner time; to make me strong; to help me to grow; Mum tells me to.* Make a list on the board.

Talk with the children about the foods they like to eat and their reasons: *they taste good; they are special treats; we have this to eat when we go out.* Add their responses to the list. (There may be children in your class who cannot eat certain foods because of allergies or their family's religious beliefs, so ensure that any discussions on diet are handled sensitively.)

Discuss the foods that they do not like. Have they been told these are good for their health? Should they eat things which are healthy even though they may not like them? Ask the children for their reasons for not liking them. Point out that some foods are promoted as 'healthy' in advertisements and that this can sometimes influence our choices.

40 mins **Development**
Provide the children with a selection of pictures of foods cut out from magazines. Ask them to sort these into foods that they think are healthy and foods that they think are unhealthy, working in their groups. This will generate discussion and possibly some disagreement, but emphasise that they must come to a group decision for each food. Ask the children to label the foods that they think are good for them with a smiley face and those that are not with a sad face. They can do this by standing their label in front of the group of pictures.

Give two large sheets of card to the children and ask them to paste down all the foods in the smiley face group onto one sheet and all the foods in the sad face group onto the other. Explain that each child should then choose at least one food that they like and one that they dislike, writing their name on a self-adhesive label (and adding the word *likes* or *dislikes*) and placing it next to the appropriate pictures.

Talk with the children about who decides what they eat at home. Do they have opportunities to choose meals for themselves? If so, what influences their choice? Do they choose the same

Learning objectives
● Learn how to make simple choices that improve their health and well-being.
● Understand that choosing certain foods can help us to be more healthy.

Lesson organisation
Teacher-led, whole-class discussion with visual stimulus; individual and group activities; plenary.

Vocabulary
eating
drinking
hungry
taste
smell
appearance
healthy
nutritious

sort of foods that they see other children eating? Do they want their parents and carers to buy food that they have seen in advertisements in magazines or on television? Be aware that there will be many children who have limited opportunities to decide on meals for themselves, but there may be times when they can influence the choices their parents and carers make. Encourage the children to give you feedback about when they have been able to choose what to eat or what not to eat. They may say things such as *at home in the evenings; at school; at the supermarket at weekends; for my lunchbox; when we went out to eat.*

Now provide the children with sheets of paper to draw and record occasions when they have chosen food for themselves, for example:

I chose an apple for my lunch.
I chose my own take-away.
I chose a brown bread sandwich.
I chose beans and chips for tea.

15 mins **Plenary**

Display the pictures of food that the children have sorted and pasted onto card and discuss the selections they have made. Which is the most popular food? Which category is it in – the 'healthy food' category or the 'unhealthy' one? Are there any foods that have not been labelled with anyone's names? Encourage a positive approach to healthy eating, pointing out that diets that are good for you have less fat, sugar and salt in them.

ICT opportunities
A data handling package could be used to present the results of the group work, showing the children's likes and dislikes. This would then take the form of a class survey.

Follow-up activities
● Younger children could set up their own pretend health shops in which they choose healthy foods to buy, or their own cafés in which they provide a menu of healthy options for customers.
● Invite a person who helps to prepare school lunches to talk to the children about providing a healthy, balanced menu so that they can choose food that is good for them.
● Ask the children to watch advertisements for food on television and record whether each one is for 'healthy' or 'unhealthy' food. What sort of balance is there between the two?
● Suggest that the children find out more about foods that are good for them from books and leaflets. Are they surprised by the range of foods?
● Give the children some healthy eating recipes, for example cakes made with organic wholemeal flour and sweetened with honey instead of sugar, to try out at home with their parents and carers.

Differentiation
Less able children may need help to find and select appropriate pictures for each category. Encourage more able children to justify the choices they have made regarding healthy and unhealthy food, for example *I have placed this picture of a cake in the unhealthy group because it is covered in sticky icing and has a lot of sugar in it.* In addition, invite them to provide reasons for their likes and dislikes of certain foods.

Assessing learning outcomes
Are the children able to recognise healthy food, distinguishing it from food that is less healthy? Are they aware of the necessity to make the right choices about food, so that they are eating food that is good for them? Do they understand that what other people choose to eat and what they see in advertising can influence their choices?

 How can I look after myself?

What you need and preparation

Prepare a box containing a selection of products that are put onto the body, for example soap (and water), shampoo, ointment, suncream. You will also need: a large picture of a clothed child (with a border around the picture for the addition of labels); Blu-Tack; an empty box; small pieces of paper; photocopiable page 122; writing materials.

What to do

Introduction
30 mins Show the children a large picture of a child and discuss what the child is wearing – articles of clothing, shoes and so on. Ask the children what else might go onto their bodies. Invite them to think of a variety of situations: when they get up in the morning; when they are out in the hot sun; when they are out in cold weather in the winter. Write down each suggestion on a blank label and fix the labels with Blu-Tack around the figure of the child, for example soap, water, suncream, sunhat, lipsalve.

Develop the discussion by asking them to consider times that they might fall and hurt themselves. What might need to be put on their skin? What about other situations, such as when they are having their hair washed. What might they put on their faces if they are going to a party? Label the picture with other products – disinfectant, ointment, plasters, shampoo, face glitter, face paint and so on. Talk about other things that can get on our skin – dust, dirt, mud, crayon – and add those to the picture.

Look at the labelled picture together and ask the children: which things are good for our bodies and which things should we remove? Establish that the first category would include products such as soap and ointment; the second would include things such as dirt and crayon. Which of the things make us feel good? Which make us feel not so good? Help the children to understand the link between helping ourselves to stay clean and free from infection and helping ourselves to feel confident.

Learning objectives
● Understand that keeping their bodies clean helps to protect them from infection.
● Recognise that maintaining personal hygiene can improve their confidence and self-esteem.

Lesson organisation
Teacher-led discussion with visual stimulus; individual/group activities; plenary session.

Vocabulary
clean
wash
hygiene
dirty
bathe
protection
soap
shampoo
dirt
mud
dust

Development
40 mins Organise the children into groups and provide each group with small pieces of paper. Show the children a box containing products we put on our body that are 'good' for us, for example soap, shampoo, protective creams, ointment. Explain to the children what these products do to keep us healthy, to make us feel better or protect us from infection. Invite the children to suggest other things that might go in the box.

Hold up an empty box for the children to see. Ask them to think of things we put on our body that

What I can do for my body

The children could produce drawings and sentences of their own about looking after their bodies using a graphics package on the computer.

Follow-up activities
● Ask the school nurse or other healthcare worker to visit the class to talk to the children about personal care.
● A group of children could design a calendar which has reminders about healthy habits on it for each month. They could add their own cartoon drawings.

need to be removed in order to keep us clean and healthy. (Refer to the labels around the picture of the child, if necessary.) Invite the children in their groups to write on the pieces of paper things like paint, mud, dust, dirt, face paint. Explain why these should be removed. Ask them if they can think of anything dangerous that they have been told to keep away from, for example bleach and garden products like weed killer. They could add these types of products to their suggestions.

Now place all the pieces of paper in the box. Ask them to label the box *Must be removed*. Label the box that you used in the introductory part of the activity *Good on our bodies*. Invite the children to suggest symbols that could be used to go on both types of box.

Give out copies of photocopiable page 122 and ask the children to look at the pictures and to write about each one. They must think about what they would do in that particular situation to look after themselves. What would be needed for their body to protect them from something (whether it be the sun, dirt – it is up to them to decide)? For example: *On the beach the sun was very hot, so I put some suncream on; I fell and hurt my knee, so I had the dirt washed off and some cream put on it to stop it hurting; My dog licked my hands, so I had to wash them before I had my tea; My hair was dirty, so I had it washed with some shampoo to make it clean again.*

10 mins Plenary
Discuss the importance of establishing good hygiene habits, doing things regularly, perhaps at a set time. Talk about any routines the children have for themselves, and reaffirm the connection between knowing how to look after yourself and feeling good about yourself.

Differentiation
Support less able children in their completion of photocopiable page 122 by providing them with key words that relate to the pictures, or asking an adult helper to scribe what they wish to say. Encourage more able children to give extended answers, developing further reasons for keeping clean or protecting their bodies. For example, for the 'cut knee' picture they could mention that the wound would need to be cleaned to get rid of germs and to prevent the risk of infection.

Assessing learning outcomes
Do the children understand that there are reasons for applying some substances to our bodies and removing others? Do they appreciate that looking after their bodies can improve both their health and their self-esteem?

1 hour 10 mins Have you ever been ill?

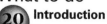

Learning objectives
● Understand that some illnesses can be caught, but can often be controlled by taking the necessary action.
● Realise that medicines can make them better, but can be harmful if they are not used properly.

What you need and preparation
You will need: A3 sheets of thin card, suitable to make two class Big Books, paper (for illustrations in Big Books); strips of paper (for writing in Big Books); glue; writing, drawing and colouring materials.

What to do
20 mins Introduction
Talk to the children about what it is like to feel ill. Ask them:
● What sort of things have happened to you?
● Did you look ill? How did you look?

- Did you have to stay in bed?
- Did you visit the doctor or did the doctor visit you?
- What hurt? How did you feel?
- Who looked after you?

Using A3 sheets of card, record the children's experiences. Leave spaces for the children to add their own illustrations at a later date. Give the front cover the title: *When I was ill...* This can then be followed by the children's responses, such as:

I cried a lot.
My head hurt.
I felt tired.
I had lots of spots.
The doctor came and took my temperature.
My skin hurt.
I had to stay in bed.
I was sick in the night.
My tummy hurt.

Read the sheets of shared text together and explain to the children that these will be made into a special class book and that they will draw pictures to illustrate the writing.

Invite the children to describe what made them feel better. Ask:

- Did you stay in bed?
- Did you have to take some medicine?
- Who came to visit you?
- Did you have special treats? What were they?

Explain to the children that they are going to write and illustrate a second special class book, *We felt better when...*

30 mins Development

Provide each group with strips of paper to complete a page of the book. Encourage them to write as many different reasons for feeling better as they can think of:

I had a long sleep.
I went to hospital and the nurses looked after me.
I took medicine every day.
My gran bought me a present.
My mum looked after me.

Paste each group's responses onto sheets of card, and provide time for the children to illustrate their writing. Then collate the pages of the book and read them as a whole-class activity.

20 mins Plenary

Show the children some of the pages for the first Big Book, *When I was ill...* again. Do they know why they might have become ill? Did anyone they know have the same illness?

Lesson organisation
Teacher-led discussion; whole-class activity involving shared writing and reading; group activities; plenary session.

Vocabulary
illness
doctor
nurse
medicine
thermometer
temperature
tablets
stethoscope
surgery

What I can do for my body

ICT opportunities
The Big Books could be made using a desktop publishing package, with the children's own drawings scanned in onto the appropriate pages.

Follow-up activities
● Ask the children to draw pictures to accompany the text in the *When I was ill...* Big Book, completed in the introductory session.
● For younger children, set up a role-play area as a doctor's surgery, with a bed, stethoscope, toy thermometer, empty medicine bottles (plastic), dressing-up clothes and so on.
● Suggest that the children produce drawings and words of advice about what to do when you are ill which would be suitable to put up in the waiting room of a doctor's surgery, for other children to read.
● Invite the children to devise their own safety rules about medicines, to be displayed on the classroom wall.

When they had a sore throat, did anyone else also have a sore throat? What about when someone in the class had chickenpox? Where did it come from? Did anyone else catch it? Do they think we can pass on illnesses to each other? Establish that illnesses can be caught from someone else but that we can do things to make this happen less. For example, we can stay at home when we have chickenpox or poorly tummies; wash our hands often; don't cough or sneeze near other people.

Now look at some of the collated sheets for the second Big Book, *We felt better when...* Focus on the taking of medicines to make us better. Who should always have charge over medicines? Stress the importance of only taking medicines when they are given by a doctor, nurse, parent or other adult whom they know. Why should they never swallow anything they find in bottles, jars or packs of pills? Where should medicines always be kept? (There will be times when children need to take medicines themselves, but only when they have been trained how to do so, for example inhalers.) Do they know what would happen if they took too much medicine or swallowed too many tablets?

Sum up by saying that we all become ill sometimes; we can help to avoid spreading illnesses, however; medicines can help to make some illnesses better, but we must never take them on our own; medicines are dangerous if not used properly.

Differentiation

Less able children may need to discuss possible reasons for feeling better with an adult helper before they write their text for the Big Book, *We felt better when...* Invite more able children to write their responses on card themselves, in the introductory session when you are compiling the pages for the Big Book, *When I was ill...* You could also encourage them to develop their ideas about the spread of some illnesses: *I had a cold. My sister had a bad cold, too. I caught it because...; I had chickenpox. Everyone on my table had chickenpox. I think this happened because...*

Assessing learning outcomes

Do the children understand that there are many common illnesses that are spread by contact with other people? Are they aware that there are ways of reducing the spread of these illnesses? Do they understand that medicines can help to make them better, but that medicines can be dangerous if they are not used properly?

Building healthy environments

This chapter adopts a broad interpretation of the term 'environment'. It encompasses the physical and social environment which children grow up in, together with a range of subjects and issues related to it. As children get older they will increasingly experience the pressures of various aspects of their environment and be influenced by them. However, it should be recognised that children themselves have a part to play in shaping certain aspects of their environments, whether it be at home, at school or in their local community.

The activities in this chapter seek to develop children's understanding of building a 'healthy' environment. This can relate to the natural world – to the countryside and the habitats of plants and animals, for example – and also to the quality of life within the physical environment, including such things as personal safety and protection of possessions. Throughout the chapter, the overriding aim is to help children develop a sense of responsibility, ownership and commitment to both the physical and social dimensions of their environment.

The issue of personal safety and behaving responsibly is important so that children do not put themselves or others at risk. It also links in with the idea of choice and how positive behaviour and attitudes affect the quality of our environment in a way that is beneficial to all.

CHAPTER 3

Keeping myself safe

This unit is designed to help children think about aspects of their own personal safety. It introduces them to various contexts in which they should consider their safety as important and encourages them to think about what they might need and should do (and not do) in order that their personal security is not jeopardised. The aim is to give children the knowledge, skills and self-confidence to approach situations and the ability to respond appropriately. It is also to heighten children's awareness of risk, but without frightening them and heightening their insecurity.

They are introduced to the idea of what 'being safe' actually means and their feelings when they either feel safe or not. They are encouraged to think about safety rules and the reasons for them, whether they be indoors or outdoors. They are introduced to simple strategies that are designed to help them handle unexpected situations, for example becoming lost or ill.

In a careful and supportive manner, they are also given the opportunity to think about places or incidents which might be considered dangerous and things they might do to avoid finding themselves exposed to those experiences. They are asked to describe the features which make them dangerous and, if possible, how they could be made less dangerous.

They are given the opportunity to consider that people as well as places can make them feel unsafe. Suggestions are offered not only for what they might try to do to avoid such incidents, but also for what they could do if they ever found themselves faced with people who are a threat to their personal safety and well-being. The children are also invited to consider what the feelings of other people might be if someone close to them was put at risk.

The subject of play and its associated dangers is also tackled in this unit, since accidents can be caused by activities involving 'play'. The children are asked to consider safe and unsafe places to play as well as safe and unsafe forms of play. From an early age, children can begin to deal with the concept of risk and how to assess it in simple terms. In this unit opportunities for discussion are provided in which you will be able to help the children to explore the relationship between fun, enjoyment, excitement and risk – everyone at some point in their lives takes risks, but it is the measure of the risk which is the difficult skill.

The role for the teacher is a very sensitive one in this particular topic and most teachers will be aware of the ways in which the children can (or can't) cope with such issues. The balance is between giving the children the all-important self-confidence and self-assurance to be able to handle particular potentially difficult experiences, not creating these to such a degree that they feel able to take needless risks. There is also a balance to be struck between the realisation of danger, and possibly in the process heightening children's worries, and playing down the risks. The teacher's sensitivity to the needs of individual children is paramount.

UNIT: Keeping myself safe

Enquiry questions	Learning objectives	Teaching activities	Learning outcomes	Cross-curricular links
Who am I?	• Recognise that it is valuable to share their opinions on things that matter. • Understand that it is important to think about themselves and to learn from their experiences. • Know that it is important to remember their address and telephone number and be able to tell a responsible person the full name of an adult in their family.	Teacher-led discussion about feeling safe and unsafe in different situations. Guidance to children about what to do if they are lost. Individual activity: completing a record sheet giving personal details including home address and telephone number.	Children: • know the name of an adult in their family who is responsible for them • remember their addresses and telephone numbers • are aware that this knowledge is important for their personal safety	English: organising information
Is it safe?	• Understand that actions which mean that they are taking risks can be very harmful to themselves (their own bodies) and others. • Recognise that it is important to think carefully about particular actions, without doing them on the spur of the moment or because they see others doing them.	Whole-class discussion about situations which involve risk and possible injury. Paired activity in which children judge how dangerous particular actions are, followed by discussion. Group brainstorming about safe and unsafe places, with results compared.	• appreciate the idea of risk and danger to themselves and others • see that in some situations it is important to make decisions themselves • recognise the importance of the feelings of their parents and carers when deciding on a course of action • have the confidence to be able to use this awareness • understand that sometimes people take risks or do dangerous things to raise their own self-esteem	English: sharing ideas and experiences
How can I keep safe?	• Realise that having opinions on things that matter is important. • Understand that they should try to deal with their feelings in a positive way.	Analysis of pictures relating to safety by whole class. Individual recording about places and situations that are 'safe' or have potential danger.	• recognise that some places or situations are safe and that others can be dangerous • understand and assess risk to their personal safety in different situations	English: communicating to others in writing, explaining their views
What are the risks?	• Recognise that there are different types of danger.	Teacher-led discussion about the risks that children may encounter in their daily lives. Individual activity in which children draw different types of dangers and write appropriate slogans.	• recognise that there are different types of danger • distinguish between situations which are dangerous because of risks *they* might take and those created by other people	Science: recognising that there are hazards in electrical appliances, and taking action to reduce the risk to themselves and others.
Are we safe indoors?	• Understand that it is necessary to learn how to recognise dangers. • Realise that dangerous places and situations can be familiar ones rather than unfamiliar.	Whole-class discussion about what to remember when playing indoors. Children sharing their ideas in groups about where they like to play and what their games are. Making zigzag books about indoor play.	• are aware that familiar places can be as dangerous as unfamiliar ones • identify which places and situations are dangerous and assess the level of risk	English: writing an explanation of how to play a game.
Are we safe outdoors?	• Recognise that dangers can be found outdoors.	Listing safe and unsafe places to play outdoors, through discussion. Individual activities: children painting a favourite place outdoors where they like to play; assessing risks of different situations and recording how they keep themselves safe.	• recognise risks that might be present if they do not consider their safety outdoors • provide safety solutions so that they can play happily and safely outside.	English: imaginative writing about a dangerous and mysterious place.

Keeping myself safe

50 mins Who am I?

Learning objectives
● Recognise that it is valuable to share their opinions on things that matter.
● Understand that it is important to think about themselves and to learn from their experiences.
● Know that it is important to remember their address and telephone number and be able to tell a responsible person the full name of an adult in their family.

Lesson organisation
Teacher-led discussion; individual activities; plenary session.

What you need and preparation
You will need: index cards with names, addresses and telephone numbers of all the children in the class; board or flip chart; photocopiable page 123; an enlarged map of the locality; writing, drawing and colouring materials.

What to do
15 mins Introduction
Introduce the topic of 'feeling safe'. Ask the children:
● When do you feel safe?
● What are the things that make you feel safe? (When you are with other people? When you know a place well?)
● What feelings do you have in these situations? (Happiness? Comfort? Feel relaxed?)

Talk about the meaning of the word *safe*. Ask the children for other words that could mean the same.

Develop the idea of feeling unsafe, for example when you are alone in a strange place or when you meet someone for the first time. Introduce the words *danger* and *dangerous*. Talk to the children about any experiences they may have had which relate to the idea of feeling unsafe. Handle this area with sensitivity, using their responses to draw out positive learning points – thinking carefully before acting; checking with someone else; getting someone else's opinion, and so on.

Tell the children that now you are going to introduce yourself to them, giving them the details they would need to know if you were in a certain situation. They will have to guess what the situation is. Say something similar to the following: 'Hello. My name is... I live at... My telephone number is... My children's names are...' Ask the children why they think you introduced yourself in that way. Did they guess that you were lost?

Now ask them:
● What would an adult need to know if you ever got lost?
● What would the important points be?
● Why is it important to know who we are?
● Is there anything I could have added of importance when I gave my own details?

Record the children's responses on the board. Tell them that being able to give information like this to an adult will help them if they ever get lost.

Is there anything else they can tell you about safety when they are away from their house and family? What safety rules are they given? Emphasise that keeping safe is about 'knowing' and 'understanding' the importance of certain information. Keeping safe is about making good, sensible choices.

25 mins Development

Ask the children if they can remember their name, address and telephone number. Have to hand the school's pupil record cards with their addresses and telephone numbers on them, for children who cannot remember, and show them to the class to point out that there is often another contact number on the card, such as a parent's work number. Why do they think this is important? When might this information be used?

Provide each child with a copy of photocopiable page 123. Explain that they should draw a picture of themselves and write their name, then draw their home and write their address and telephone number. Invite them also to draw their family and write down their names. Remind the children about what you talked about at the beginning of the activity, if necessary, before they write their answer to *If I got lost, I would do this…*

Vocabulary
safe
unsafe
home
school
family
friends
address
telephone

10 mins Plenary

Select a few children to show their completed photocopiable sheets to the rest of the class. Reinforce the importance of knowing where they live and being able to give their full name and address. Do the children also know the name and address of their school?

Display a large street map of the locality. Invite the children to identify where they live, naming their road or street. Can they find their way from a friend's house to their own? Can they find safe ways to travel to and from their house? What dangers are there if they ignore safety rules?

Differentiation

Provide less able children with their addresses and telephone numbers, to help them complete photocopiable page 123. An adult helper could scribe for them, if necessary, and also discuss with them what sorts of things they would do if they got lost, helping them to record the information on the sheet. Encourage more able children to think of additional information about themselves to add to the back of the sheet.

Assessing learning outcomes

Do the children know the name of an adult in their family who is responsible for them? Can they remember their addresses and telephone numbers? Are they aware that this knowledge is important for their personal safety?

ICT opportunities
The children could input information about themselves at the computer, using their completed photocopiable sheets for reference, but using their own layout ideas.

Follow-up activities
● Ask the children to compile a list of safety rules to be remembered when they are away from home, for example *Always cross the road carefully – stop, look and listen; Never try a different route that you do not know, if you are walking to school or to a shop on your own; Say no to strangers; Always go back to the classroom, if you are being collected from school and there is no one there; Wear something bright if you are out at night; Tell someone in your family if you are going outside to play; Make sure that people always know where you are,* and so on. The rules could be displayed on a poster on the classroom wall.
● Younger children could use role-play in pairs to practise phoning home to tell an adult where they are.

CHAPTER 3

**Keeping
myself safe**

 Is it safe?

What you need and preparation
You will need: photocopiable page 124 (enlarged); board or flip chart; paper; writing and drawing materials.

What to do

25 mins Introduction
Introduce the topic of safety by using the word *risk*. Ask the children if they know what it means and if they can give you examples of what 'taking a risk' means, for example playing with matches, playing near the road, lighting fires. Move on to talking about the 'risk of what...?' – getting yourself hurt, causing damage, hurting someone else and, worse, of getting permanently injured or even killed. Extend the discussion so that the children understand that taking risks is potentially dangerous both to themselves as well as others.

Show the children an enlarged copy of photocopiable page 124 and discuss each picture in turn. Is it showing an action that is dangerous in the sense that a person could get hurt? Ask the children to work in pairs to decide whether what the child is doing is 'very dangerous', 'quite dangerous' or 'not dangerous at all'. Invite some of the pairs to give feedback to the rest of the class. Establish that all the scenes show something that is potentially dangerous.

Ask the children if they have ever done anything which they would describe as risking harm to themselves. Maybe they climbed up a tree and got into difficulties. Have they ever been hurt because they were doing something that was dangerous? Ask them if they have ever considered doing anything dangerous and decided against it – why did they choose not to do it? Talk to the children about the possibility of someone else trying to persuade them to do something dangerous and how important it is to say no.

20 mins Development
Divide the children into small groups and ask them to discuss the idea of 'safe' and

'unsafe' situations. What makes a place safe? What makes it unsafe? Nominate one child in each group to write down their group's thoughts. Explain that each group must make a drawing of each of these places and write key words and phrases underneath it. For example, a 'safe' place could be their home; an 'unsafe' place could be the park at night.

When the children have finished, ask each group to team up with another group to look at each other's drawings and compare their ideas. Are there any things which are similar? What is safe or dangerous about the places? Are any dangerous actions being undertaken in the unsafe places? Do any of the pictures show other people as potentially dangerous?

Plenary

15 mins Discuss the idea that it is very important to think carefully about our own actions, as well as actions which other people might try to persuade us to take that may risk our safety. Tell the children that one question they might ask themselves if they are faced with a potentially dangerous situation is: 'Would my mum and dad [or other carer at home] be happy if they knew I was going to do this?' Point out to the children that knowing that someone else would be very concerned about you can help you to say no. It can give you the strength not to take risks even though to your friends it might 'look good' to do otherwise.

Differentiation

Less able children may need help with their drawings of 'safe' and 'unsafe' places by being provided with clues to help them to think of ideas. More able children could produce a simple storyboard which shows a sequence of three or four pictures in which the dangerous elements of an unsafe place are demonstrated.

Assessing learning outcomes

Are the children able to appreciate the idea of risk and danger to themselves and others? Are they able to see that in some situations it is important to make decisions themselves rather than to follow what their friends think they should do? Do they recognise the importance of the feelings of their parents and carers when deciding on a course of action? Do they have the confidence to be able to use this awareness as a gauge for knowing what to do (or what not to do)? Are the children able to understand that sometimes people take risks or do dangerous things to raise their own self-esteem?

Follow-up activity
The children could design their own 'safety highway code' for children relating to 'safe' and 'unsafe' places.

How can I keep safe?

What you need and preparation

You will need: board or flip chart; photocopiable pages 125 (enlarged copy) and 126; writing materials.

What to do

Introduction

15 mins Show the children an enlarged copy of photocopiable page 125. Explain that it has pictures of places and situations which could be dangerous, and talk about each one in turn – the busy street, the train station, the beach, the funfair, the swimming pool, the football match, the play area, the riverside path. Study each picture together and discuss what the risks to people's safety might be. What would it be important to remember? For example, on the riverside path it would be essential not to walk too close to the edge. Record the risks and the 'rules' on the board.

Learning objectives
● Realise that having opinions on things that matter is important.
● Understand that they should try to deal with their feelings in a positive way.

**Lesson
organisation**
Teacher-led
discussion;
individual
activities; group
activity; plenary
session.

Vocabulary
safe
unsafe
danger
secure
risk

20 mins Development

Distribute copies of photocopiable page 126 and ask the children to draw a place that they know is 'safe' and a place that they think is 'dangerous'. They must then try to think of how the place could be made 'unsafe' (for their first drawing) or 'safe' (for their second drawing). Encourage them to give reasons for their choices, for example *My safe place is my home. It would be unsafe if there was a flood, and water started coming into the house.* Or: *This is where people can go for walks at the seaside. It is on the cliff tops and I would not feel safe. There should be a barrier to make it safe.* Some children may focus on dangers which are very real to them in other ways, for example *In the school playground I sometimes feel scared of the bigger children – they make it feel dangerous. To make it safe I think there should be a separate playground for us.* The children can continue on the back of the sheet.

10 mins Plenary

Allow the children to share their views and feelings on safe places and dangerous places. Are some places more dangerous than others? Encourage them to give feedback about how they think their dangerous places could be made safer. If their remedies cannot be put into action, how will they deal with the place that is dangerous to them? What if the unsafe place is caused by people rather than the place itself? Do they feel that they have fears that they hope to grow out of, for example a fear of dogs or spiders?

Differentiation

Provide adult support for less able children so that they can discuss what would be appropriate for them to focus on when they are completing the photocopiable sheet. A few key words relating to their chosen situations would also be helpful to them. Suggest that more able children draw and write about two places for each category rather than one. In their dangerous places, what actions would they take to keep themselves safe?

Assessing learning outcomes

Can the children recognise that some places or situations are safe and that others can be dangerous? Are they able to understand and assess risk to their personal safety in different situations?

**Follow-up
activity**
Ask a safety
'expert', for
example a police
officer, into school
to talk to the
children or to be
interviewed by
them.

What are the risks?

What you need and preparation
You will need: board or flip chart; large sheets of paper; writing, drawing and colouring materials.

What to do

Introduction
15 mins Discuss what the children have learned about keeping safe. Recap on the meaning of *dangerous*. Can the children think of other words which mean the same? They may suggest words such as *unsafe, risky*. Talk about the meaning of risk, focusing first on things, then on places and people. For the first category, explain that using dangerous things without considering safety can cause them to be at risk. What kinds of things should they never touch? What kinds of things can they use, but only with great care? For the second category, what kind of place could they go to that could put them at risk? Encourage them to think first about the familiar, then the less familiar. Finally, are they ever at risk with people? Make sure that the children are aware of the danger of strangers and that they are not expected to trust a person whom they don't know. Talk about other 'people' dangers such as being in a large crowd where it would be easier for them to get lost or being alone with a bully (take the opportunity to tell the children that they must always tell someone else if they are being bullied, so that the person can make sure that they get help).

Make a list on the board, as the discussion develops, so that you have three headings, with appropriate ideas under each one relating to 'risks', for example:

Things
boiling water
hot saucepans
knives
fires

Places
busy roads
disused buildings
parks
rubbish dumps
building sites

People
bullies
strangers
crowds

At the end of the discussion, distinguish between risks that they may take themselves, such as using things inappropriately or going to unsafe places, and risks that are posed by others, such as a stranger who might approach them.

Learning objective
Recognise that there are different types of danger.

Lesson organisation
Teacher-led discussion; individual activities; plenary session.

Vocabulary
dangerous
unsafe
safe
risk
brainstorm
hazard

CHAPTER 3

Keeping myself safe

ICT opportunities
Ask the children to key in their slogans at the computer. These can then be printed out, cut to size and pasted underneath their 'danger' drawings.

Follow-up activities
● Ask the children to work together in groups to write a simple poem or jingle that presents the message of 'Safety first'.
● Invite a police liaison officer to come in to school to talk to the children about the danger of strangers and to offer them advice about what they can do to keep themselves safe from people they don't know.

(30 mins) Development
Provide each child with a large sheet of paper and ask them to write the headings *Things, Places* and *People* across the top. Invite them to draw a possible danger under each one, then write a slogan – *Don't touch; Keep away; Tell a grown up;* or *Run away*, for example.

(5 mins) Plenary
Remind the children that they have considered different kinds of danger. Reinforce the point that they can take responsibility for managing some risks, for example only crossing the road if it is safe to do so, not playing with sharp knives, not talking to strangers.

Differentiation
Encourage less able children to refer to the lists on the board for ideas about what to draw for each category ('Things', 'Places' and 'People'). It may be appropriate for them to focus on just one category rather than three. An adult helper could scribe their slogans for them. Invite more able children to give reasons for their slogans, for example *I have written 'Don't touch' because this object is used for cutting and it is very sharp.*

Assessing learning outcomes
Can the children recognise that there are different types of danger? Are they able to distinguish between situations which are dangerous because of risks *they* might take and those created by other people?

(1 hour) Are we safe indoors?

Learning objectives
● Understand that it is necessary to learn how to recognise dangers.
● Realise that dangerous places and situations can be familiar ones rather than unfamiliar.

Lesson organisation
Teacher-led discussion; whole class, group and individual activities; plenary session.

What you need and preparation
You will need: board or flip chart; blank zigzag books; A4 paper; pack of self-adhesive red spots; a set of prompt cards (each card with *Who? What? How? Where?* or *When?* written on it); glue; writing, drawing and colouring materials.

What to do
(15 mins) Introduction
Remind the children about some of the safety issues discussed in the previous sessions and the importance of keeping safe. Explore with them what they enjoy doing when they are indoors at home, at school or when they visit other people's houses. Do they play? What do they play? Where do they play?
Talk about the games they like to play at home or at a friend's house, then ask:
● Do you play safely?
● What can make play dangerous?
● Are there any rules for playing indoors?
● Are these different from ones for playing outside?
● Do they depend on the people whose house you are playing in or the people with whom you are playing?
Make a list on the board of all the places where the children play indoors. Discuss which places might be dangerous, for example playing on the stairs; in the kitchen; in a garage or garden shed where there are dangerous tools.

Development

30 mins Organise the children into groups and provide each group with a set of prompt cards: *Who? What? How? Where?* and *When?* Ask the children to discuss together for five minutes the places indoors where they enjoy playing. Encourage them to talk about *who* they like to play with, *what* they like to play, *how* they play (if it is a game, what are the rules?), *where* they play (does it need to be in a special place?) and *when* they play (for example, morning, evening, afternoon, weekend, weekday).

After the children have shared their ideas, give out some sheets of A4 paper and explain that they are going to make a zigzag book about indoor play; each child is going to contribute a page. Invite them to draw a place indoors where they enjoy playing and to draw themselves playing there. They should use half the paper for their picture, then write a description of their play, referring to the prompt cards if necessary, to remind them of the ideas they discussed in their groups.

The completed pages can then be collated and pasted into a zigzag book, one for each group. Invite the children to write a title on the front page, for example *Do we choose safe places for our play?*

Plenary

15 mins Give each group an opportunity to talk about the play described in their zigzag book and to show the rest of the class their pictures. Ask them which places or ways of playing might be dangerous. What are the risks? Where are the risks? Who could cause a risk? How could an accident happen?

Provide each group with some self-adhesive red spots. Ask them to put a red spot on the pages that show a dangerous place or a dangerous situation. They can then extend this by analysing the level of risk: 'a little dangerous' can be given one spot, 'quite dangerous' three spots and 'very dangerous' five spots.

Review the places and activities that are shown and encourage the children to consider how likely it is that an accident might happen and why. If there are books without any red spots at all, congratulate the groups on playing safely!

Differentiation

Less able children may need to describe their play, using the Who? What? How? Where? When? format, to an adult helper who could scribe for them. Encourage more able children to think about how their own actions could make a situation potentially dangerous when they are playing, and to include their ideas in their zigzag books.

Assessing learning outcomes

Are the children aware that familiar places can be as dangerous as unfamiliar ones? Are they able to identify which places and situations are dangerous and assess the level of risk?

Vocabulary
safe
unsafe
risky
dangerous
accident

Follow-up activities
● Ask the children to focus on one area indoors, for example the kitchen, the bathroom, the garage, and make a list of potential hazards.
● What activities are forbidden in their homes or in other people's homes to make them safe indoors? Who says 'No'? Why do they think they say 'No'? Would they like to be able to do these activities? Why would they like to do them? Discuss this with the children.

 Are we safe outdoors?

**Learning
objective**
Recognise that
dangers can be
found outdoors.

**Lesson
organisation**
Teacher-led whole-
class discussion;
individual
activities; plenary
session.

Vocabulary
safe
unsafe
risky
dangerous

What you need and preparation

You will need: photocopiable page 127; board or flip chart; paper; writing, drawing and art materials.

What to do

15 mins Introduction

Remind the children of the previous activity in which they focused on their play indoors and any inherent dangers. Explain that they are now going to think about their play outdoors. Discuss where the children enjoy playing and make a list of the places on the board. Ask them:
● Where are the safest places to play and explore?
● What makes these places safe?
● Where are the unsafe places to play and explore?
● What makes these places more dangerous? What must you not do there?
● Can safe places also be exciting places?

Now ask the children if they have been given any rules for playing outside. Make a list of these on the board.

45 mins Development

Provide the children with paper and art materials and ask them to draw or paint a place outside where they like to play. Encourage them to show whether they are alone or with other children, with family or other adults. If there is time, they could draw or paint a place to which they would not go because they feel it is too dangerous.

Now give out copies of photocopiable page 127 and separate sheets of paper. Look at the middle section of the sheet together and explain that the children have to think of dangers that there might be in three different places: the playground, the park and the street. Give them examples, such as the concrete surface in the playground if they fall over, a deep pond in the park, busy traffic in the street. Ask the children to write a danger for each area, then use the text in the small boxes as prompts to write or draw about what they do to keep themselves safe. Box 4 is for a place of their own choice.

Follow-up activities
● As a class, look at the rules that the school has to keep children safe outdoors, for example no going out of the school gate at playtime; not playing with hard balls in the playground; walking sensibly in pairs if out on a school trip.
● Ask the children to make up a modern-day fairy tale which features a dangerous and mysterious place that the characters must keep away from if they are to remain safe.

10 mins Plenary

Display the children's pictures and invite them to talk about what they have drawn or painted. Where is the place? Who is there? Are there any risks involved in being there? Share the risks and dangers that they have identified on photocopiable page 127.

Differentiation

Support less able children by helping them to identify risks when they are outdoors and to record their answers on the photocopiable sheet. More able pupils could extend their answers to compile an advice leaflet about keeping safe outdoors.

Assessing learning outcomes

Are the children able to recognise risks that might be present if they do not consider their safety outdoors? Can they provide safety solutions so that they can play happily and safely outside?

Taking care of our possessions

In this unit the focus is on possessions – a part of a child's environment which can be very important to some children, but less so to others. At a very young age, a child might become attached to a comfort blanket or a teddy bear (and be distraught at the loss of the item!), or might not have an overdependence on any object. As children become older, whether possessions are important to them or not, they can be helped to develop a responsible attitude towards them and to learn how to look after them. They can also begin to realise that if they can be trusted to look after things of their own, they will be trusted to look after other people's, which will help them to develop into reliable young adults.

When things are stolen, people feel aggrieved and emotions run high. If children's own possessions are stolen they have to learn to cope with exactly the same feelings. They need to be reassured that there are people who can help them in such circumstances – that they are not alone. It is also possible to help children to try to understand possible motives for such behaviour as well as appreciating the consequences of such actions. Possessions can be stolen even though every step has been taken to minimise the risk, but children need to be aware that, nevertheless, it is important to develop responsible behaviour for their own part; and if they are given the correct guidance and encouragement, they will have the self-confidence to deal with such experiences if they should ever occur.

UNIT: Taking care of our possessions

Enquiry questions	Learning objectives	Teaching activities	Learning outcomes	Cross-curricular links
What is a valuable possession?	• Recognise that possessions may be valuable for a variety of reasons; different people value them for different reasons.	Whole-class discussion about valued possessions. Paired discussions about special items. Game played in groups, with children creating imaginary stories about particular items.	Children: • explain why an item is valuable to them • are aware that there may be a variety of reasons for items being valuable • appreciate other people's ideas of what is valuable	English: presenting ideas to an audience.
How do we look after our possessions?	• Learn to take and share responsibility. • Understand that valued possessions need to be looked after carefully.	Teacher-led discussion about ways in which individual possessions are looked after, followed by paired activity on same theme. Group activity based on caring for different objects and living things. Feedback from children in order to compile a class list.	• appreciate that it requires discipline and a routine if things are to be looked after and taken care of properly • appreciate the consequences of not looking after possessions	Science: understanding how to treat animals with care and sensitivity.
What happens when possessions get lost?	• Understand that it is important to know how to describe possessions in case they get lost. • Realise that losing possessions is sometimes beyond their control.	Introductory focus on lost items and problems that may arise. Children describing a favourite toy that they imagine they have lost. Group and paired activities: children describing items in order for them to have a chance of being found. Giving accurate descriptions of other people.	• appreciate the importance of being able to describe items in the case of them getting lost • express their feelings about losing their possessions • understand that people react to the loss of possessions in different ways	English: giving accurate descriptions.
What if my possessions are stolen?	• Recognise that people steal for a variety of reasons. • Understand that stealing harms everyone, including the person who steals.	Teacher-led discussion about stealing. Paired activity explaining possible reasons for thefts occurring in different situations. Comparison of responses and compilation of revised list of reasons.	• appreciate that people choose to steal for different reasons • who have had things stolen themselves express how they felt about such behaviour • link together the situations shown in the storyboard	Art and design: responding to text by drawing ideas.
Who can help?	• Learn to take and share responsibility. • Understand that people can help them when things get lost.	Sharing experiences of losing things. Group story about a lost item. Individual activity in which children explain who they would ask for help in certain situations.	• identify people who could help them in different situations • understand that this means that they are learning to take responsibility for their possessions.	English: explaining and sharing ideas.

55 mins What is a valuable possession?

What you need and preparation
Make sets of object cards by copying photocopiable page 128 onto card and cutting out the cards (one set for each group). You will also need: board or flip chart; writing materials.

What to do

20 mins Introduction
Introduce the idea to the children that we all have objects or items which we care about very much – they are possessions which we value and like to look after. They could be birthday presents or perhaps things we have collected on holiday or been given for a special occasion, such as when we first went to school. Ask the children for examples of their own precious things, and list them on the board.

Organise the children into pairs and ask them to think of one item each that is special to them. Ask them to tell each other why the item is special to them – the occasion on which they received it or bought it, how long they have had the item, and so on. Encourage each child in the pair to ask their partner one or two questions about their special possession.

Now invite individual children to say something about their special possession to the rest of the class. Talk to the children about value in relation to money. How many of the things they chose were expensive? Was money an important factor in making the item valuable?

25 mins Development
Divide the children into groups and give each group a set of object cards (each card with the name and picture of an object that could be regarded as valuable on it) made from photocopiable page 128. Ask each group to play the game 'What's the story?': the players take it in turns to pick up a card, say the name of the special object and make up a little story of why this object was of special value to someone (for example, the cricket bat, seen in the photograph of the boy, could have been given to the boy as a present when he was taken to see England play a test match). Encourage the children to be imaginative in their ideas.

10 mins Plenary
Discuss the idea that we do eventually change our opinions about what we count as our valued possessions. Ask the children if they can think of things that they once valued but have now changed their minds about.

CHAPTER 3

Taking care of our possessions

Talk to the children about their views and opinions of what other people regard as valuable. Can they appreciate that what others regard as valuable may be different from their own views?

Follow-up activities
● Invite the children to bring items of value to them into school and display them on a table in the corner of the classroom. Stress the importance of asking their parents and carers first, and make sure they understand that the item does not have to be valuable in terms of cost. The display could be titled *What's the story?*
● Ask an older group of children in the school to talk to the class about their valuable possessions in order for the younger children to appreciate how what they value can change.

Differentiation

In the game 'What's the story?' less able children may need an adult helper to offer them some key sentences to guide them in their story based on their object card. Encourage more able children to use their oral stories as a framework for a written story about a treasured possession and its owner.

Assessing learning outcomes

Are the children able to explain why an item is valuable to them? Are they aware that there may be a variety of reasons for items being valuable? Are they able to appreciate other people's ideas of what is valuable?

① How do we look after our possessions?
1 hour

Learning objectives
● Learn to take and share responsibility.
● Understand that valued possessions need to be looked after carefully.

Lesson organisation
Teacher-led discussion; paired task; small group activity; plenary session.

Vocabulary
care
time
thought
responsible
worth
valued

What you need and preparation

Make sets of picture cards by copying photocopiable page 129 onto card and cutting out the cards (one set for each group). You will also need: photocopiable pages 129 (enlarged copy) and 130; board or flip chart; large sheets of paper; writing materials.

What to do

② Introduction
20 mins

Introduce the idea that if we value our possessions we have to take responsibility for looking after them if they mean that much to us. This means taking the time to do things such as using them carefully, asking others to use them carefully if they are sharing them and putting them away safely after using them.

Ask the children if they can think of any other ways in which their possessions can be looked after.

Show the children an enlarged copy of photocopiable page 129. Can they think of ways in which these people would need to look after their possessions? Ask them to give you their suggestions, and write them on the board. For example, *To look after her car, the woman will need to make sure that there is enough petrol and oil, keep it clean and have it checked regularly.*

Give out copies of photocopiable page 130 and ask the children to draw and write about how they look after a special possession.

Development

 Divide the class into small groups and give each group a set of picture cards made from photocopiable page 129. Explain that their task is to take it in turns to select a card and the group must then work together to think of all the ways in which they would take care of the object (or living thing) shown on the card. One child should write down the suggestions on a large sheet of paper.

Encourage the groups to share their ideas and to see if they agree with each other's suggestions for looking after the special possession. Is there anything they would want to add to the list? Compile a class list of all the suggestions, for display.

Plenary

Invite individual children to show their completed copies of photocopiable page 130 to the rest of the class and to talk briefly about what they have drawn and written. Discuss the idea that people have to take responsibility for taking care of their things. This often means giving up our time and setting aside other things we might want to do in order to give our full attention to the task. Talk about the consequences of not looking after things, for example what would happen if the car or the plant (see photocopiable page 129) were not looked after? Why is it sometimes hard to take responsibility for caring for our possessions?

Differentiation

Help less able children with their writing about their own possession on photocopiable page 130 by providing them with key words and phrases to complete the sentences. Encourage more able children to think of special possessions that other people might have collected, for example an explorer, and to write a few sentences, using the format given on the photocopiable sheet.

Assessing learning outcomes

Are the children able to appreciate that it requires discipline and a routine if things are to be looked after and taken care of properly? Are they able to appreciate the consequences of not looking after possessions?

ICT opportunities
The children could key in their list of 'caring tasks' on the computer (see Development), once they have made a collaborative list on rough paper.

Follow-up activities
● Encourage the children to talk to other teachers or their parents or carers about how they look after their special possessions.
● Make a special class book containing examples of the children's work.

What happens when possessions get lost?

What you need and preparation

You will need: lost property box containing different items (ensure that it contains some unusual objects or toys as well as sweatshirts, vests, gloves and so on); photocopiable page 131; paper; writing materials.

What to do

Introduction

Show the children the lost property box and take out the items, discussing how they may have got lost. Why have they not been claimed? Do some of them look the same? (A problem if articles have not been named.) Talk about some of the more unusual items. Are they more likely to be claimed by their owner? Why do the children think that is?

Invite a few of the children to describe a favourite toy. Ask them to imagine that they have lost it and they are trying to explain what it looks like to someone who has never seen it before

Learning objectives
● Understand that it is important to know how to describe possessions in case they get lost.
● Realise that losing possessions is sometimes beyond their control.

CHAPTER 3

Taking care of our possessions

Lesson organisation
Teacher-led discussion; paired activity; small group activity; plenary.

Vocabulary
missing
lost
upset
sad
description
find
replace

and is going to help them find it:

● What is it?
● What size is it? Is it large or small?
● What colour is it and what material is it made of?
● Has it got any special marks or missing bits?

Encourage them to tell you why it is their favourite toy and how they would feel if they lost it. Would they feel angry, sad or worried, for example? Help the children to be aware of how people can react to the loss of something in different ways. Some people don't mind if things get lost, but others can be extremely irritated or angry. Explain that this is because they feel that they have lost control. However, that's what losing things is about; we lose things even though we do not mean to. If something gets lost, we have to accept that even though we might try very hard to find it again, we might not.

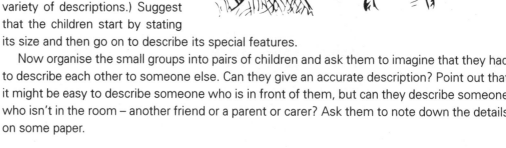

(25 mins) Development
Divide the children into small groups and give each group a copy of photocopiable page 131 and a sheet of paper. Ask them to imagine that one of the items on the sheet was missing – their task is to give a full description of it, to help it to be found. (You may wish to assign different objects to different groups to ensure a variety of descriptions.) Suggest that the children start by stating its size and then go on to describe its special features.

Now organise the small groups into pairs of children and ask them to imagine that they had to describe each other to someone else. Can they give an accurate description? Point out that it might be easy to describe someone who is in front of them, but can they describe someone who isn't in the room – another friend or a parent or carer? Ask them to note down the details on some paper.

ICT opportunities
Ask the children to produce a drawing and a description of the missing possession (or the person they are describing) at the computer.

(15 mins) Plenary
Describe one of the items on photocopiable page 131 and see if the children can guess what it is. Invite them to share their own descriptions that they wrote down in their groups. Can the other children in the class guess what the items are and do they think that they are clear and accurate?

Encourage the children to talk briefly about how they feel when something that they have lost is found. They may feel relieved and happy, but has it altered how they feel about their possessions? If they feel that it was partly their own fault that the object got lost, will they look after things differently next time?

Differentiation

Help less able children with their description of the missing item (see Development) by suggesting a few specific clues relevant to the item. An adult helper could scribe the details, if necessary.

More able children could choose more than one object to describe.

Assessing learning outcomes

Are the children able to appreciate the importance of being able to describe items in the case of them getting lost? Are they able to express their feelings about losing their possessions? Are they able to understand that people react to the loss of possessions in different ways?

Follow-up activity
The children could go on to create an imaginary story, told from the point of view of the item lost.

55 mins What if my possessions are stolen?

What you need and preparation

You will need: photocopiable pages 132 (plus an enlarged copy in order for the pictures to be cut out for display) and 133; board or flip chart; paper; writing and drawing materials.

What to do

20 mins Introduction

Begin by talking to the children about stealing. Establish that stealing means taking something that does not belong to you, taking it without asking, and keeping it without the intention of giving it back. Discuss the difference between stealing and borrowing. Ask the children if they have ever had anything stolen from them:

- What was it?
- Was it valuable?
- Do they know how it happened?
- How did they feel when it happened? (For example, did they feel very angry towards the person who had done it, or were they angry with themselves for letting the person take their possession?)

Learning objectives
● Recognise that people steal for a variety of reasons.
● Understand that stealing harms everyone, including the person who steals.

Lesson organisation
Teacher-led discussion; paired activity; group discussion; group activity; plenary.

Vocabulary
stolen
theft
crime
jealousy
poor
suffer
benefit

Record some of the children's responses on the board.

Talk to the children about why people steal. Perhaps they are short of money and see it as an easy option. Perhaps there is something they particularly want that they cannot see themselves getting any other way. Explain that it is not always easy to pinpoint specific reasons; it may be a way of life that people 'fall into' without thinking first about the consequences.

Divide the class into pairs and give each pair a copy of photocopiable page 132. Ask them to think of possible reasons for the people in the pictures stealing the objects. Organise the pairs of

ICT opportunities
The storyboard could be produced on the computer, with clip-art images incorporated.

Follow-up activities
● Help the children to act out the storyboards in a simple drama.
● Ask them to improvise a conversation between someone who has stolen a piece of property and the person from whom it has been stolen.

children into small groups of four or six and ask them to compare their responses. Give out some sheets of paper and explain that they must make a small group list, to be displayed alongside the pictures.

25 mins **Development**
Give one copy of photocopiable page 133 to each group and explain that their task is to produce a simple story in pictures using the outline provided on the sheet. Read through the text for each box with the children before they take turns to draw an appropriate picture. Make sure that they discuss what the content of the last box should be before a picture is drawn.

After they have produced their storyboard, ask them to join up with another group and share and explain what they have done. Encourage each group to ask a question about the other's storyboard.

10 mins **Plenary**
Discuss with the children the idea that crimes like stealing have consequences for the criminal and their families. They can, of course, get caught – this will affect their families as well as themselves. Sometimes they may meet up with other people who steal, and then it can become even more serious, with bigger crimes being committed. They may even become victims themselves.

Talk about what sorts of things they think should happen to people who steal, such as being sent to prison, being made to pay back what they stole, and so on.

Differentiation
Less able children may need help with both activities, but particularly photocopiable page 133. Discuss possible ways in which they could illustrate the sentences. Encourage more able children to add more detail to the text to 'flesh out' the story, writing on a separate sheet of paper.

Assessing learning outcomes
Are the children able to appreciate that people choose to steal for different reasons? Are children who have had things stolen themselves able to express how they felt about such behaviour? Are they able to link together the situations shown in the storyboard?

1 hour Who can help?

Learning objectives
● Learn to take and share responsibility.
● Understand that people can help them when things get lost.

What you need and preparation
Find one or two story books which involve situations in which the characters ask for help because they have lost something, for example *This is the Bear* by Sarah Hayes and Helen Craig (Walker Books). You will also need: photocopiable page 134; paper; writing materials.

What to do
30 mins **Introduction**
Remind the children of the earlier activity they did about losing something precious (see 'What happens when possessions get lost?' on page 65). Share their experiences of losing something – being unsure where the lost item might be, wondering where to get help, and so on. How do they try to explain how they feel? Encourage the children to talk about who they would ask and what they would do if they lost a special possession.

Now read a story to the children about a character losing something and asking a person for help. In *This is the Bear* the boy's dog pushes his bear into a dustbin and the bin is immediately carried away by a man who has come to collect the rubbish; the boy, alarmed and worried, goes to the dump and asks a man there to help him find his teddy bear; the man has no luck in finding the bear, but it is eventually found by the dog. Emphasise that this is only a story, but in real life the children need to know who to ask for help when something is lost, so that if they cannot find the item themselves they can be guided by people who may be able to help them.

20 mins Development
Provide each child with a copy of photocopiable page 134 and read through the problems given at the foot of the sheet. Ask the children to look at the pictures and identify which people they would ask to help them with each problem. Point out that it does not matter if there isn't a picture of the person they would ask; the pictures are only there to give them ideas. They can then draw the person for each situation on a separate sheet of paper. (They may choose more than one person for a situation, if appropriate.) Encourage them to include drawings of friends, family, teachers, school helpers and other members of the community. Finally, ask the children to write a caption which explains the picture they have drawn, for example *This is my teacher, Miss O'Neill. If I could not find my PE bag, I would ask her to help me.*

10 mins Plenary
Invite the children to share their ideas about who they would ask to help them in each situation. Look for any significant differences, and point out that knowing who to ask for help when things get lost will allow them to take some responsibility for their own possessions.

Differentiation

Help less able children with their work based on photocopiable page 134 by discussing possible options for each situation. Reassure them that there are no 'right' and 'wrong' answers. Encourage more able children to think of other problem situations, together with solutions, and to draw and write about them.

Assessing learning outcomes

Are the children able to identify people who could help them in different situations? Do they understand that this means that they are learning to take responsibility for their possessions?

Lesson organisation
Teacher-led discussion and whole-class story; individual activities; plenary session.

Vocabulary
safety
helpers
special
risk
protect

Follow-up activities
● Brainstorm with the children any messages that different people give them about looking after their possessions. Can they remember them all? For example, *Always put your bike away. Remember to hang up your coat. Put CDs back in their cases.* Identify with the children two or three messages that they think are the most important. Display these in the classroom.
● Ask the children to create a series of 'advice posters' for children to read if they have lost a valuable possession, for example *1. Keep calm! 2. Think about when you last saw the item. 3. Try and look for it yourself, if you think you lost it at home or at school. 4. Ask someone to help you find it...*

Building healthy communities

As young children's social and cultural development takes shape within the context of the classroom, school and the wider community, they will increasingly encounter issues, problems and challenges which will require the application of both a knowledge and understanding of society and the skills required to cope with the evermore complex sets of relationships of which they will become a part. In particular, as government guidelines for PSHE and citizenship indicate, supporting children's cultural development involves helping them to understand the nature and role of the different groups to which they belong.

Young children's ability to operate effectively as members of different groups grows in importance throughout Key Stage 1 – it is here that the building blocks of effective co-operation, collaboration and mutual respect for one another are built. It is also at this point that there is a growing realisation that success, both in intellectual and social terms, depends on the children's ability to build and maintain their position within a group.

Understanding how different groups work, appreciating the need to adapt to different types of groups and realising the overriding value of the group in terms of the successful attainment of a community's goals are all important stepping-stones towards children's social and personal development.

Working as a member of a group is also a context within which attitudes and values are formed and shaped. At the heart of group membership lies the notion of responsibility, not only to the group as a whole but to the individuals within it, to the 'task' and, last but not least, to themselves. No less important is the need for respect and empathy in one's dealings with others, not only for the sake of the successful achievement of the 'task' but also the equally essential goals of group cohesion and stability.

Effective communication skills lie at the heart of most successful groups – an ability to listen, to argue, to present, to reiterate are just some of the skills upon which group processes depend. These are key skills which all children need to develop in as wide a variety of contexts as possible, including that of personal, social and health education.

Paradoxically, groups need individuals. No group in which every member has an identical set of skills, the same knowledge base and matching attitudes will succeed. Groups need the variety brought by individual strengths (and weaknesses). Children need to be helped to understand that being a member of a group does not invalidate their individuality. It does, however, require self-discipline and self-control to manage one's own individuality within the context of the group. Groups in which that self-discipline is absent within its individual members will fail. Children have to have the experience of succeeding (and failing) in the safe environment of the classroom in this important area of social development.

This chapter begins to address this all-important agenda for children of this age, that of learning to be a part of a larger unit, of no longer being the sole determiner of one's success and no longer the single object of other people's time and attention.

My class, my school

This unit takes the concept of the 'group' as the basis for the development of a healthy community; the concept of the 'group' is explored through such areas as the class, the school and the wider community. The unit also examines the idea of leadership within the group and the skills and attributes required of a good leader.

The children are asked to consider what the term 'group' means and how it applies to their experiences. They are asked to think about such things as the sharing of common goals and reasons for why the group came together in the first place. Children of this age will have limited experience of working in a group, though they may well be familiar with playing in a group. Increasingly, however, there will be expectations on them to work effectively in groups. The focus of the activities in this unit is on group working to complete a task, with the importance of maintaining the social cohesion of the group being recognised.

The unit emphasises certain key skills for group work: activity 2 focuses, for instance, on the skill of communication, activity 3 on the skills of leadership and activity 4 on the skills of decision-making and prioritising. These are important generic skills which all children are required to develop and use, and the activities provide them with practice and experience in these areas.

UNIT: My class, my school

Enquiry questions	Learning objectives	Teaching activities	Learning outcomes	Cross-curricular links
What is a group?	• Learn that they belong to various groups and communities, such as family and school. • Recognise that there are many reasons for groups being formed. • Understand that there are important skills needed for groups to work well.	Whole-class discussion about the nature of a group. Identification of different types of group. Paired activity: children sharing their ideas about what they do in groups and how they work together.	Children: • identify a range of group types • appreciate the idea that groups of people can live, work and play together effectively	Mathematics: gathering data and organising information.
How do we work together?	• Develop a sensitivity to the needs and feelings of others. • Develop an awareness of how individuals interact in group situations. • Learn to work effectively in small groups.	Teacher-led discussion about how the class functions as a group. Group activity: playing a game which requires co-operation between members. Follow-up analysis of how successful the game was.	• appreciate the importance of groups having rules to work to • appreciate the purpose of the game – that is, to look out for the needs of other people • talk about how they felt while the game was being played	English: interacting within a group to make a task successful.
Who's in charge?	• Recognise the need for authority and rules and understand how rules help them. • Recognise that in a group or community different people have different responsibilities to make the community a happy 'healthy' place (environment).	Exploration of what being in charge means. Group reading of a poem about responsibility. Discussion about different tasks that people undertake within a group in order for things to run smoothly. Group activity: children imagining what they would do if they were the teacher for a day.	• understand what being responsible means • relate it to experiences of their own • consider other people's responsibilities and what they would do if they had to take over being in charge	Science: selecting group leaders to prepare for a science investigation, setting out equipment and resources; discussing how well they fulfilled their responsibilities.
Can we have an adventure?	• Agree and follow rules for their group in an imaginative situation. • Consider the effects of acquiring and sharing resources.	Discussion about what life would be like on a primitive island and how they would survive. Group activities: choosing essential items to take; working out responsibilities for different group members; devising a list of rules; role-playing their daily life.	• appreciate the need for organisation and structure in the group • appreciate that people have different strengths and capabilities • work together effectively to decide on procedures	English: devising rules, recording and discussing them before producing a definitive set for the group; shared reading of stories focusing on the theme of working together.
Is our school a community?	• Understand that they have responsibilities as members of a group to the wider community. • Agree and follow rules for their group and classroom, and understand how rules help them.	Identifying different groups within the school. Discussion of school rules and why they exist. Group activity: recording of children's views about school rules.	• appreciate the importance of rules in a community • gather and analyse the information effectively • appreciate that there was a range of attitudes towards the rules.	English: discussing the importance of 'positive' behaviour strategies.

(45 mins) What is a group?

What you need and preparation
You will need: class photograph (optional); pictures of different types of groups (football teams, ballet classes, children working on a task together – any group involving a collection of people); board or flip chart; photocopiable page 135; paper; writing and drawing materials.

What to do

(15 mins) Introduction
Introduce the concept of a group by talking about the class as a group. You could show the children a class photograph of themselves, if available. Ask them:
- What is a class?
- Is a class a group?
- Why do you think it is? (Or why don't you think a class is a group?)
- Do groups have to be small or can they be big?
- Can groups just have two people? Is a couple a group?
- What do you think a group is?
- Do groups have to be organised?

Tell the children that you want them to help you to record the groups they think they know. Record their ideas of what a group is on the board: *A group can be… the people on my table; my family; the Saturday football club; the Brownies with our leader on a trip; our class; the audience at a concert; just me and my friend.* Show them some pictures of different types of groups, and add the ones that have not been thought of already to the list.

Encourage the children to consider what groups do together, for example play, work, relax. Do people in groups behave differently from how they behave if they are working or doing things on their own?

(20 mins) Development
Organise the children into pairs and provide each pair with a copy of photocopiable page 135. Invite them to work together to share ideas about groups to which they belong. Explain that they should choose one group to focus on, when they complete the sentences.

When the pairs have completed the task, ask them to join up with two other pairs to compare their sheets. Ask the children to find out if they appear on other class members' lists (see the first question). Do their ideas about what makes their group work differ in any way?

Now ask the groups to answer the following questions:
- How does the group stay together?
- Has the group changed its members?
- If someone has dropped out of the group, what were the reasons?

(10 mins) Plenary
Discuss the advantages and disadvantages of being a member of a group. Talk to the children about the size of groups – what number do they think makes for a good working relationship?

Learning objectives
- Learn that they belong to various groups and communities, such as family and school.
- Recognise that there are many reasons for groups being formed.
- Understand that there are important skills needed for groups to work well.

Lesson organisation
Whole-class, teacher-led discussion; paired and group activities; plenary session.

Vocabulary
individual
couple
group
skill
collection
organised

Follow-up activity
Ask the children to assign special tasks to different groups in their class, for example they could think about who would be best for a group to show a visitor around the school or who would be best for a group to look after the school's environment area.

Differentiation

Ask less able children to draw a picture of a group that they are part of and give it the caption: *This is me in my _____ group.* Encourage more able children to sum up their feelings about being part of a group, once they have completed the photocopiable sheet. Do they prefer to be in small groups or large groups? They could record their thoughts using the format: *I like working with a partner because...* or *I like working in a group because...*

Assessing learning outcomes

Are the children able to identify a range of group types? Are they able to appreciate the idea that groups of people can live, work and play together effectively?

40 mins How do we work together?

Learning objectives
● Develop a sensitivity to the needs and feelings of others.
● Develop an awareness of how individuals interact in group situations.
● Learn to work effectively in small groups.

Lesson organisation
Whole class, teacher-led discussion; group activity; plenary session.

Vocabulary
individual
group
need
share
co-operate
process

What you need and preparation

Make a selection of cards (picture postcards, Christmas cards and so on), one for each child and therefore the exact number for each group. These should be cut into four to six simple shapes and each piece marked with a code to identify the group. Take the cards to be used by Group A. Mix up the pieces and place the identical number of pieces in an envelope for each child. Code the envelopes *Group A*. Repeat this process for each group. Code the envelopes. You will also need: board and flip chart; a strip of card for each child; writing materials.

What to do

15 mins Introduction

Encourage the children to talk about what they have found out about groups, reminding them of the previous activity, 'What is a group?' Help them to think of what the class does as a group together – lessons, activity sessions, PE and games, playing outside, going on school visits. How do they think the class works together? What do they need to do to make the class successful as a group?

Record their responses on the flip chart, for example *not shout out, listen, be kind, share, wait our turn, follow instructions first time, be ready,* and so on. Most classes will have a code or set of rules which should support the children in identifying what they know is appropriate behaviour within the class group, whether in or out of school, for example no running in the corridors.

Ask the children to consider how well they think they can do all the things they have suggested.

(10 mins) Development

Tell the children that they are going to test their skills in working together as a group. Place in front of each child an envelope containing sections of card. Ensure each group has the same coded set of cards. Instruct the children not to touch or open their envelope.

Explain to the children that the task is for each group to complete a set of pictures made from pieces to be found in the envelopes in front of each child. Go through the rules of the game: the game must be conducted in silence; no one must speak; no one must ask for someone else's piece of card; no one must point; no one must grab; everyone must look and see what other people need. Players can pass pieces of card from their envelope to other players. They must help each other to complete all the pictures.

Invite the children to open their envelopes (in silence) and place the pieces of card face up in front of them. Encourage them to look at their pieces of card and those in front of the others in their group. Who has most pieces of one picture? Can they see anyone who might need a piece from their envelope to help complete the picture? Remind them that they are all helping each other.

Note any children who are particularly good at considering the needs of others. Note those who find the co-operative task difficult. Keep reminding them of the rules.

After about ten minutes, or earlier if finished, stop the task. (Check for pieces dropped on the floor!) Ask the children how successful they have been. What went well? What did they find difficult? How well could they work together?

(15 mins) Plenary

Remind the children of all the suggestions they made prior to the activity, and display the list on the flip chart. Ask each group in turn to consider what they were good at or not so good at from the list of previous suggestions. Without implying success or failure, encourage the children you previously noted in the development activity to contribute to the discussion. Are there any other things they have learned about working together in a group? Add their comments to the list on the flip chart.

On the board, write the heading *Working in a group means…* Provide each child with a strip of card and ask them to write down one thing they have learned about working in a group – *listen, share, help, co-operate, think about others, don't argue, be kind,* and so on. Use the children's ideas to make a list of points to remember when working in a group. Display the list in the classroom.

Differentiation

Put more able children into larger groups or give them pictures that have more pieces to fit together. Less able children could work in pairs on simpler pictures with fewer pieces.

Assessing learning outcomes

Are the children able to appreciate the importance of groups having rules to work to? Are they able to appreciate the purpose of the game – that is, to look out for the needs of other people? Are they able to talk about how they felt while the game was being played?

ICT opportunities
The children could produce a set of illustrated school rules on the computer, for display.

Follow-up activity
Suggest that the children design their own game which has rules that depend on them working together as a group.

CHAPTER 4

My class, my
school

(55 mins) Who's in charge?

Learning objectives
● Recognise the need for authority and rules and understand how rules help them.
● Recognise that in a group or community different people have different responsibilities to make the community a happy 'healthy' place (environment).

Lesson organisation
Whole-class, teacher-led discussion; group activities; plenary session.

Vocabulary
in charge
rules
responsibilities
roles
group
team
resources

What you need and preparation

Find a poem or story which involves people making decisions for others and taking charge, and the consequences of ignoring sensible rules. You could use 'Disobedience' by AA Milne in *When We Were Very Young* (Methuen Children's Books), for example. You will also need: board or flip chart; photocopiable page 136; writing materials.

What to do

(25 mins) Introduction

Explore with the children the meaning of *being in charge*. Ask the children if they can think of other words or phrases which mean the same, for example *being responsible*. What do they think is involved in being in charge? Have they ever been put in charge of anything? (Perhaps a younger brother or sister, a pet, a special possession or piece of equipment, a job or activity, something in the classroom.) Who put them in charge? Did they tell them what they had to do?

Read the poem 'Disobedience' (which begins *James James Morrison Morrison, Weatherby George Dupree*), or a similar story or poem that is about responsibility. What was James's advice to his mother? *(You must never go down to the end of the town, if you don't go down with me.)* Explore the humour evoked by James's advice being ignored. Encourage the children to talk about how it feels to be in charge of something or to be given a special role or responsibility. What has happened when they have been in charge of someone (or something)? If it was a person, how did he or she respond to them? Did the person do what they asked?

How do they feel about the special responsibilities at home or in the classroom? Who is in charge of the classroom? Is it just one person – the teacher? Of what is the teacher in charge? All the children? What happens during the day? What resources are used? Are they in charge of anything that goes on in the classroom? (Their belongings, their behaviour and actions, keeping things tidy and safe.)

Ask the children to think about the idea of being in charge. What makes them feel good? What is not so good? Record on the board situations in the classroom that show that someone is in charge. Group the text under headings, for example:

Teacher	**Children**
teaching us lessons	giving out the paper
taking the register	keeping our tables tidy
getting help from classroom assistant	collecting in books
helping us with our work	picking up pencils from the floor
bringing us in from the playground	handing out the milk
making classroom rules	collecting litter
giving us instructions	
keeping us safe	

Explore with the children how this helps make their classroom 'work'. What would happen if no one took responsibility and no one took charge?

Development
20 mins Provide small groups of children with a copy of photocopiable page 136. Direct them to the ideas recorded on the board under the heading *Teacher*. Explain that their task is to look at the things listed and imagine that on one day the teacher was absent. Could they take on one (two at most) of the responsibilities? Ask them to work out which ones (or parts of) they would do and explain their reasons. Remind them that they would be doing this as a group.

Plenary
10 mins Share the ideas that the children have recorded on photocopiable page 136. Consider together the importance of joint responsibilities and what would happen to the organisation and running of the class if no one took responsibility for activities, resources and materials, and caring for people. Talk about classroom rules and the importance of making these together and keeping them together. Reiterate that everyone has a responsibility for 'taking charge' of what goes on and how they act in their class group.

Differentiation
Help less able children to identify ways in which they would carry out the task they select. Encourage more able children to think of additional responsibilities to those on the list that they could take on.

Assessing learning outcomes
Are the children able to understand what being responsible means? Are they able to relate it to experiences of their own? Are they able to consider other people's responsibilities and what they would do if they had to take over being in charge?

ICT opportunities
● Use an appropriate modelling program which involves children in a problem-solving activity in which they have to take charge.
● Word-process a list of rules and suggestions for making the class or group work effectively together, devising a way of sharing responsibilities.
● Send an e-mail to a class in a different school of children of similar age. Find out about their class organisation – what rules, roles and responsibilities do they have?

Follow-up activity
Ask the children to imagine that they could have someone's job for a day – it could be a famous person or someone who is known to them. What would their daily activities entail and how would they make sure that they were in charge? Ask them to describe and role-play a part of that job, using others in their class to help them.

Can we have an adventure?
1 hour 10 mins

What you need and preparation
Collect together the items below for a box of equipment for each group. You will also need: a bag for each group; PE mats; coloured armbands (a different colour for each group); large sheet of paper; writing materials.

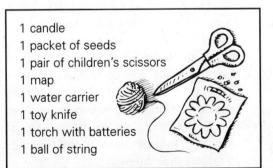

1 candle
1 packet of seeds
1 pair of children's scissors
1 map
1 water carrier
1 toy knife
1 torch with batteries
1 ball of string

What to do
20 mins **Introduction**
Explain to the children that they are about to take part in an adventure. Ask them to imagine that they are on board a ship that is about to sink. In the distance is a small island. They will just manage to wade or swim to the island before the boat sinks if they are quick.

Learning objectives
● Agree and follow rules for their group in an imaginative situation.
● Consider the effects of acquiring and sharing resources.

My class, my school

Lesson organisation
Whole-class, teacher-led discussion; role-play activity using hall or large play area; plenary session.

Vocabulary
community
group
need
considerate
co-operation
responsibility
fairness
survive

When they get to the island, their task is to work together to survive. They will have somewhere to live, something to eat, something to attract attention to get off the island and daily chores will need to be done. They will need to find out more about what is on the island, if they are to make the most of their resources. They will be working in groups but will have to work together. Remind them how they work together in the classroom and explain that they will need each other to survive on a strange island.

Organise the children into groups of four to six and provide each group with a different-coloured armband. Direct each group to a table on which you have placed a box of objects (see What you need and preparation), helpful for survival on the island. Explain that each group has three minutes to choose five useful objects from the box and place them in the bag provided. (More than five and the bag will sink in the sea and they will have nothing!) Encourage the groups to question what would be most or least useful and to try to reach agreement together.

40 mins Development

In the hall, where mats have been previously placed, ask each group to take their place on a mat. Explain that their mat and the space around it represents their island. There are trees, a stream, rocks by the shore, a mountain in the distance.

Discuss with the children the roles and responsibilities that will be needed for the people living on the island. Together, choose a role for each group: hunters, food gatherers, fire-makers, cooks, builders and so on. Give the children the opportunity to think about whether there may be any other groups that will be needed.

Then ask the children to make a list of rules with you on a large sheet of paper which all people living on the island should follow. Encourage them to make suggestions based on the idea that it is essential for everyone to work together as a group, pooling resources and dividing up tasks. Discuss the consequences of breaking the rules, asking the children to give you their ideas. For example, if they had decided that they must all share their food carefully because of limited resources and someone decided to raid the food-store one night, how would they feel about it and what would they do?

Now ask the children to role-play their life on the island, remembering the type of job that their group members have been assigned. Emphasise the importance of working together as a whole group. Are there resources or equipment that they can share or exchange? Can any groups work together? Does each group build its own shelter? What is the most important thing to do first? How are they going to construct their camp and provide facilities for their survival? Note how they are working together and whether they become involved in any conflicts – about the sharing of resources, for example. If so, are they able to resolve their differences?

10 **Plenary**
mins Draw the groups together to discuss their experiences. Did each group manage to work together to help the whole community? Did anyone break the rules? How, and was it reasonable? How should they be dealt with? What was difficult about working together? Did they share or keep their own resources? What were the reasons for this? What should happen next?

Differentiation
Less able children may need help with identifying tasks suitable for survival on the island. Start them off with key questions such as 'What will we need to do first?', then suggest scenarios that their role-plays could include, such as:
● Look, there is a boat in the distance. How can we make it see us?
● The hunters have just returned having found a village on the other side of the wood. How can we find out if the people are friendly?
● The builders want to move to another site by the mountain. Is it fair that they should go and leave us? Can we manage without them?
  During the development activity, more able children could make a list of problems that could be encountered on the island, and add possible solutions.

Assessing learning outcomes
Are the children able to appreciate the need for organisation and structure in the group? Are they able to appreciate that people have different strengths and capabilities? Are they able to work together effectively to decide on procedures?

ICT opportunities
Plans of the island and daily routines could be produced on the computer.

Follow-up activity
The children could write a report for a pretend local newspaper or for a mock presentation on television on how the group survived on the island by working very closely together and in a disciplined way.

55 Is our school a community?
mins

What you need and preparation
You will need: a set of class rules, displayed on a large sheet of paper; photocopiable page 137; paper; writing materials.

What to do
15 **Introduction**
mins Invite the children to think about the larger community to which they belong – the school. Ask them:
● What groups exist in the school? (Class groups, music groups, art clubs, games clubs, football groups, friendship groups at playtime, and so on.)
● Who is in charge of these groups?
● How are they organised? Do children choose to join themselves? Are they dependent on their abilities? What age do you have to be? Does it matter whether you are a boy or a girl?
  Now talk about the role of the headteacher. Ask the children who they think is in 'charge' of the school. What do they think his or her job is? To make the rules? To look after them? To tell them off when they break the rules? To help them when they have a problem? To look after all the children? To look after the school building?
  Ask the children if they can remember any of the school rules that they have been told. Are the rules for when they are in a particular place, such as the classroom, the dinner hall, the school entrance, the playground? Display the list you have prepared and go through each one, making sure that the children understand them. Are there any rules that they know of that are not written down? Have any of the rules been made by the children themselves? Focus on

Learning objectives
● Understand that they have responsibilities as members of a group to the wider community.
● Agree and follow rules for their group and classroom, and understand how rules help them.

Lesson organisation
Teacher-led, whole-class discussion; group activities; plenary session.

Vocabulary
rules
consequences
in charge
authority
fairness
right/wrong

particular ones, asking the children why they think they have been made, and emphasise that rules help the school to be well run and also to be a happy and safe place.

(30 mins) Development

Divide the children into groups of four or five and invite them to tour the school, under supervision, with each group having the opportunity to visit a classroom or special area to find out about different rules, roles and responsibilities. Distribute copies of photocopiable page 137 and ask them to record information they gather about other children's opinions. Explain that they need to focus on two rules initially, then find out (a) if there are any rules that children think should be changed, and (b) whether there should be any new rules introduced (if so, what?).

(10 mins) Plenary

Encourage the children to discuss their findings. Can they make any conclusions, such as which rules are important, which rules are thought fair (or unfair), which rules get broken? Do the rules apply to different actions and behaviour – how others are treated, for example? If there are any rules that they would like to see changed, why? How would they help the school to be a happier place? Are there any rules missing that should be in place? Why do some rules get broken often? Does this make them 'bad' rules? In what ways do they feel that 'good' behaviour is rewarded? Have they discovered any unwritten rules?

Differentiation

Ask less able children, who may find completion of photocopiable page 137 difficult, to select just one rule and write or draw about it, after discussion with an adult helper. Encourage more able children to think about what could be changed or improved in their school and to re-read their answers to the last section of the photocopiable sheet (if any). Can they think of new rules themselves that would contribute to their school being a safe and happy place? Ask them to continue on the back of the photocopiable sheet, if necessary.

ICT opportunities
Ask the children to input their data (see photocopiable page 137) at the computer. The results could then be made into a graph.

Follow-up activity
The children could correspond, by letter or e-mail, with another school about the topic of 'rules in the school community', sharing their data and asking for additional information.

Assessing learning outcomes

Do the children appreciate the importance of rules in a community? Are they able to gather and analyse the information effectively? Are they able to appreciate that there was a range of attitudes towards the rules?

This is where we work and live

This unit is intended to assist the children to extend the idea of 'community' beyond, their own small, social group of friends and family to the wider community, initially of the whole school. As indicated in the Government's guidelines on PSHE and citizenship, children need to acquire the understanding and skills needed to become responsible and effective members of society.

The first step in the process for this age range is to help them make sense of the places, situations and experiences which directly affect them and which, in turn, they themselves can have an effect upon. So, for instance, the classroom is their environment and the way that it is organised, the way it is resourced, directly affects and shapes their learning as well as their relationship with others in their class. In turn, the children are helped to appreciate how they can affect the 'classroom', not only in the physical sense of how they behave towards other children, to the teacher, to visitors, how they respond to the 'systems' of the classroom, its rules and procedures, but how they respond to the resources made available to them, taking care of them and being responsible for their safety.

The context of the children's learning is then extended to the school and its environs (see activity 2), so that the children can apply the same principles to a new and different setting. Questions are asked about what the school and its environment offers the children, what is good about it, how it helps them, what they would change. In turn, they are invited to consider how they might shape the environment. In what ways could they improve what they have, making it better for themselves and others? They are invited to assess the quality of their own environment and find ways to express their feelings about it.

Beyond the confines of the classroom and school, the children are invited to look at the wider community and consider what places within it shape people's lives – the leisure club, the community centre, the church, the library, and so on. These are the places which contribute to a 'healthy' community, and respect and consideration are qualities required of those who use them. In turn, of course, the people who use them can influence and shape these resources – members of the church or the club can change the ways in which these places operate. The overall aim is to help the children to appreciate that the 'community' is about people and places which interact with each other for the ultimate benefit of both.

Safety is of paramount importance to everyone in every community, whether it is related to travelling to school or work or in leisure and social activities. The extent to which the community is a 'safe' place is an indicator of its 'health'. The media regularly carries reports which are evidence of just how unsafe some communities can be for all people. Aspects of safety are explored in activity 4.

Finally, the degree of care which people show for their community is a reflection of their attitudes towards the people who live in it. Someone who vandalises trees in the park is not just damaging a beautiful resource, they are also demonstrating their lack of respect and feelings for the people who live and work in that community.

These are important issues to be examined by the children, with your guidance. Often, at this age, children care passionately for their classroom, school and local environment and are concerned when it is damaged.

UNIT: This is where we work and live

Enquiry questions	Learning objectives	Teaching activities	Learning outcomes	Cross-curricular links
What sort of environment is our classroom?	● Describe aspects of their immediate environment – that is, the classroom. ● Understand that there is a close relationship between the environment and the activities that take place there.	Teacher-led discussion of the children's immediate environment at school – the classroom. Recording of their observations on the board. Describing and labelling different areas of the classroom. Paired activity: children drawing routes to key areas on plan of the classroom.	Children: ● appreciate the importance of their environment and its connection to their daily activities. ● suggest improvements and changes which are appropriate.	Mathematics: using instructions about going left and right to follow a route. Geography: understanding plans of the classroom. History: comparing classrooms from the past with modern ones.
What sort of environment is our school?	● Analyse their school environment and understand that, like any environment, it needs to be looked after.	Children identifying the position of their classroom within the school. Surveying the school and its grounds, and providing oral answers to questions about the school environment.	● express their opinions on different aspects of their school environment ● appreciate that it is an environment that people need to look after	Geography: expressing their own views about places and environments. Design and technology: devising a plan for a specific area of the school, for example the playground.
Where are the special places in our community?	● Recognise that places can be special for different reasons. ● Understand that special places are of value to the quality of the community.	Studying photographs of places of interest in the local community. Completing starter sentences about special characteristics of the places. Teacher recording key ideas on the board about places that the children like to visit. Group activity: planning a tour for an imaginary group of visitors to their town or village, and drawing and labelling places that are included in the tour.	● recognise the value of different places in the community to different people ● appreciate the need to respect and care for the environment	Geography: identifying and describing where places are. RE: visiting a local place of worship. History: learning about a place of interest, such as the site of an old farm or factory.
How safe is our community?	● Learn that some places are more dangerous than others and why.	Whole-class discussion about busy places and quiet places in the local environment, with consideration of potential dangers. Children looking at an aerial photograph of the area and identifying where they live and their route to school. Group activity: plotting a route on a map of a journey that they know.	● understand that there are reasons for some places being more dangerous than others ● assess their area for its safety in terms of people travelling	Geography: recognising how places compare with other places; using maps and plans.
Who cares for our environment?	● Understand that it is important to value and appreciate their environment. ● Recognise the importance of people whose job it is to look after their environment, but also know that everyone has a part to play in looking after the environment.	Assessment of the quality of their local environment and how well it is looked after. Individuals completing starter sentences about different aspects of their environment. Children painting a place in their locality where people can take part in leisure activities.	● assess the quality of their own environment and appreciate elements that are beneficial to people who live there.	Geography: looking closely at own environment and recording observations; recognising how places have become the way they are and how they are changing.

 # What sort of environment is our classroom?

What you need and preparation

Find some pictures or posters of different classrooms, both past and present. *School Days* by Penny Marshall (Macdonald) has a selection of photographs showing classrooms from the past which would be particularly useful. You will also need: labels displaying words which can be used to describe different areas of the classroom and resources found there (for example, *role-play area, toy washing machine, dressing-up clothes* – include general descriptive words and phrases, such as *a clear space; a crowded area*); a classroom plan showing key areas (one for each pair of children); board or flip chart; writing materials.

What to do

15 mins Introduction

Recap on what the children have learned about how they work together as a group. Explain that they are now going to explore *where* they work together: their working environment. Discuss with the children what the word *environment* means.

Show the children some pictures of classroom interiors. What can they see in the picture? How is the classroom set out or organised? What is the same? What is different? Do children have the opportunity to move around? How much free space is there? When looking at classrooms from the past, encourage the children to point out differerences they can see, such as children seated at individual desks in rows rather than grouped at tables; boys together; girls together; an absence of technology. Record the children's observations on the board.

35 mins Development

Ask the children to sit in groups at their tables. Can they describe what they can see of their own classroom from where they are sitting? Discourage them from turning around to look behind them, so that limited perspectives will allow different descriptions to be recorded. Ask them to describe one thing that they can see, for example *I can see some labelled drawers against the wall*. Now ask the children to change places with another group from a different table. Has their view of the classroom changed? Can they see different working areas and resources?

Show the children the labels that you have prepared displaying key words relating to their classroom environment. Invite a few of the children to each read a label aloud and place it in the correct areas, for example the book corner, the board, the teacher's chair or table, the computer area. Help them to place the more abstract labels correctly, for example they could place the label *a clear space* in the carpet area, and the label *a crowded area* where there is little room to move around.

Learning objectives
● Describe aspects of their immediate environment – that is, the classroom.
● Understand that there is a close relationship between the environment and the activities that take place there.

Lesson organisation
Whole-class, teacher-led discussion; group and paired activities; plenary session.

Vocabulary
shape
space
organise
change
improve
plan
resources
environment
place

Divide the children into pairs and provide each pair with a plan of the classroom showing key areas – computer area, display table, book corner, role-play area, writing area, and so on. Invite the children to identify these areas and show (by drawing lines) how they would reach them from where they are sitting. Ask the children to mark any obstacles that they would have to avoid on the way. Emphasise that they may not be able to reach the areas by moving in a straight line.

ICT opportunities

● Ask the children to plot and programme a route from one point in the classroom to another, using a programmable toy such as a Roamer, Pixie or PIP, and avoiding pre-placed obstacles.
● Invite a group of children to use an appropriate computer program (for example, *My World*) to explore the use of space and the organisation of shapes and objects in a given area.

Follow-up activities

● Encourage the children to think about the resources that are used in the classroom. Who uses what and when? Help them to sort the resources into two groups and to record their observations in a Venn diagram labelled *We share these* and *Our teacher uses these*.
● Ask the children to tackle a redesign of their classroom, changing the existing layout and facilities.

15 mins **Plenary**
Share what the children have found out about the organisation of the classroom. What is good about it? What is not so good about it? What would they like to change and improve? What would they want to keep the same? Record their suggestions on the board, and make a list together of features that a good working environment should have. Ask: 'How can we take care of our environment, keeping it tidy and safe?'

Differentiation

Less able children may need an adult helper to assist them with the classroom plan exercise. Ask more able children to use their classroom plans to write down instructions explaining how to navigate the classroom to find particular areas or resources, for example *Turn left in front of my table, go across the room to the book corner*. They could make their instructions deliberately complicated by not choosing the easiest route.

Assessing learning outcomes

Are the children able to appreciate the importance of their environment and its connection to their daily activities? Are they able to suggest improvements and changes which are appropriate?

(1 hour 10 mins) What sort of environment is our school?

Learning objective
Analyse their school environment and understand that, like any environment, it needs to be looked after.

What you need and preparation

You will need: a plan of the school and grounds; board or flip chart; key questions about the school environment on strips of paper (see Development).

What to do

15 mins **Introduction**
Remind the children of the discussion you had with them in the previous activity about the organisation of their classroom environment and its resources, the use of space, the position of special resources, the importance of designing it for people's safety. Invite them to consider the wider environment of the school, *beyond* the classroom – corridors, the hall, the school office, and so on.

Show the children a plan of the school and ask them to identify where they are within the building, for example *This is Year 1's classroom at the end of the corridor*. Where is their classroom in relation to others within the school? See if they can identify other areas – *This is the school office; this is the display area outside Year 4; this is the door to the playground*, and so on.

This is where we work and live

Ask the children if they know how to get to different areas shown on the plan. Looking at the plan, how would they reach them? Divide the children into pairs and ask one child in the pair to give directions to the other as a 'visitor'.

40 mins **Development**
Tell the children that they are going to undertake a tour of the school and the school grounds. Divide them into groups and remind them of the rules regarding moving about the school and creating a happy environment by considering the needs of others. Invite the children to consider the following questions on their tour (give each group one or two questions – each one written down on a strip of paper – on which they can give feedback to the rest of the class in the plenary):

- How easy is it to find your way about?
- Are there any signs to help you to know where to go?
- Is it obvious where classrooms and special areas are?
- What do notices around the school tell us? Do they give us good messages or not so good?
- What is displayed on the walls?
- Do you feel safe inside your school?
- Are there visitors in the school?
- What do you think is good or not so good?
  In the grounds, ask the children to notice:
- Have you space to play and spread out?
- Where are your special places?
- What do the school grounds look like? Do they make the school a welcoming place? How tidy are they?
- Do you have quiet areas and areas where you can run?
- Do you feel safe in your playground?
- What places are you not allowed to go to and why?

5 mins **Plenary**
On returning to the classroom, give each group an opportunity to give their responses to the question(s) they were given. What were their observations on finding their way around; do they think the school has a welcoming atmosphere…? Encourage the children to mention anything else that occured to them about the school and grounds.

Discuss what improvements they think could be made to their school working environment, if any. Do they think it is looked after well? How are they responsible for their environment? (Not dropping litter, and so on.) Who else takes responsibility for looking after their environment? (The caretaker, for example.)

Differentiation

Make sure that less able children are given questions that can be tackled more easily, when they are on their tour of the school. In a discussion before the tour, encourage more able children to think of appropriate questions themselves to consider.

Assessing learning outcomes

Are the children able to express their opinions on different aspects of their school environment? Do they appreciate that it needs to be looked after?

Lesson organisation
Whole-class, teacher-led discussion; paired activity; survey of school environment in groups within whole class; plenary session.

Vocabulary
plan
space
area
environment
change

ICT opportunities
The school plan could be drawn on the computer using a graphics package.

Follow-up activities
● Ask the children to produce their own plans of the school, then compare them with the plan you showed them at the beginning of the activity. How accurate are their unaided plans? Have they been able to remember the layout of the school?
● If there have been recent changes or developments to the school environment, highlight these on the school plan. Discuss with the children why the changes have been made.
● Ask younger children to paint a picture of a place that they like or don't like within the school environment. They could add a caption: *This is my favourite place because…* or *This is my least favourite place because…*
● Invite the children to design posters to display around the school which encourage pupils, staff and visitors to take care of their environment.
● The children could use any contacts they have with other schools to compare environments.

CHAPTER 4

This is where we
work and live

① Where are the special places in our community?
hour

**Learning
objectives**
● Recognise that
places can be
special for
different reasons.
● Understand that
special places are
of value to the
quality of the
community.

**Lesson
organisation**
Teacher-led,
whole-class
discussion; group
activities; plenary
session.

Vocabulary
care
spoiled
place
value
respect
vandal

What you need and preparation
You will need: a map of the locality; photographs or drawings of places in the community (see Introduction); board or flip chart; paper; writing and drawing materials.

What to do
㉒ Introduction
Show the children photographs of 'special' places in their community and point out where they are on a map of the locality – park, church, mosque, war memorial, library, museum, and so on. Remind them of the activity 'Which places are special to me?' (see page 15), if it has been carried out, as it has links with this activity. Talk to the children about why these places would be special to particular people. Ask them to try to finish the starter sentence: *This place would be special to a person because…*

Now ask them which places in the community they like to visit themselves. Encourage them to give reasons, for example *I like to visit the park with my mum and my friend because I really enjoy playing there.* What do they do in these places? Read? Play? Think? Just be quiet? Make a lot of noise? Record their ideas on the board. Discuss how they would feel if they saw these places damaged? If somebody had vandalised their play area, for example, so that they couldn't use the swings and slide, how would they feel? Emphasise that if places are allowed to remain 'special' it is of value to the whole community.

㉚ Development
Divide the children into small groups and set them the task of planning a tour for a group of visitors to their town or village. Ask the group to decide where they would take them – which places do they think would be of interest? Is it because the place is exciting or unusual? Is it because it is somewhere where they can be entertained? Ask the children to draw a series of pictures (one picture for each location) connected by lines which show the direction of the tour. Encourage them to label their pictures.

㉿ Plenary
Invite the children to share their ideas for tours. What would the visitors like about the tours? Why would they be a success?

This is where we work and live

Differentiation

You could influence choices of location for the tour by telling the children that the visitors are very interested in historical sites; sporting activities; the wildlife and natural habitat; are very keen walkers/ramblers, and so on. This would be helpful for less able children as it would provide a focus by limiting the number of places that it would be appropriate for them to include. More able children could add written information to their drawings to produce a small tour guide.

Assessing learning outcomes

Are the children able to recognise the value of different places in the community to different people? Do they appreciate the need to respect and care for the environment?

> **ICT opportunities**
> Ask the children to devise a tour of their local environment using a simple graphics package on the computer.

> **Follow-up activity**
> Ask younger children to draw four special places in their town or village which they think would be of interest to someone their age from another area.

 ## How safe is our community?

What you need and preparation

You will need: aerial photograph of the local area; plan of the local area for each child; writing materials.

Help the children to prepare for the development section of this activity by asking them to talk to their parents and carers about journeys that they take regularly – routes to work, for example. It would be helpful if they could draw a rough plan for them.

What to do

20 mins Introduction
Identify particular features of the local environment with the children – shops, garages, parks, cinemas and so on. Go through each one in turn and discuss whether they think the place is busy or quiet. Focus on the busy places. What makes them busy? (Cars, lorries, cyclists, people rushing to get jobs done, work being carried out at building sites, and so on.) Discuss different elements and establish that busy places can often be dangerous, with people having to be extra vigilant about their safety. Now focus on quiet places. Can quiet places ever be dangerous? Talk about how people need to consider ways of keeping safe in quiet places too, such as when they are near rivers and lakes. Golf courses can be dangerous in thunderstorms because you are out in a wide open space. A quiet country road can be just as dangerous as a busy road in town if you are cycling carelessly in the middle of it without thinking of the possibility of a tractor suddenly coming round the corner.

Look at an aerial photograph of the area together. Can the children identify where they live? Can they work out their route to school? How far do they have to travel? Are there any sections that they think are dangerous? If so, why are they dangerous? How do they travel? Talk about how learning about your local environment is easier if you are walking or cycling than if you are in a car on a bus.

Do they see things on their route to school which have been put in place to make people's journeys safer? (For example, bridges over busy roads to helps pedestrians cross easily.) Are there people on their route to school who help them to be safe? (For example, the crossing patrol.)

30 mins Development
Divide the children into groups and give each child a copy of a plan of the local area. Ask the children to chart a route taken by another member of their family, or a carer, on the map,

> **Learning objective**
> Learn that some places are more dangerous than others and why.

> **Lesson organisation**
> Whole-class, teacher-led discussion; individual activities within groups; plenary session.

> **Vocabulary**
> protect
> secure
> place
> care
> value
> environment
> busy
> safe
> dangerous

CHAPTER 4

This is where we work and live

using the information they have been given, if available. Alternatively, they could use their own route to school or to a friend's house.

Invite the children to consider whether the route they have marked is mainly in a busy area or a quiet area. Encourage them to record their views on whether the journey has parts that are more dangerous than others.

10 mins Plenary
Discuss with the children how important 'getting around' is for people: travelling to school, to work, to visit relations or friends, to go to the shops, to travel to take part in sport and leisure activities. People depend on all forms of transport and trust that their journeys will be safe. Encourage the children to talk about whether they would change anything about their local area for travelling.

Differentiation

Make sure that an adult helper is present to give advice to any children who need help with the plotting of a route on their map. Encourage more able children to chart a second journey on the map of a route familiar to them that is taken by someone they know.

Assessing learning outcomes

Are the children able to understand that there are reasons for some places being more dangerous than others? Can they assess their area for its safety in terms of people travelling?

1 hour Who cares for our environment?

What you need and preparation

You will need: photographs showing different areas and features of the locality; aerial photograph of local area (optional); paper; drawing and writing materials.

What to do

10 mins Introduction
Encourage the children to share what they have learned about their immediate environment in school and at home. Show them some photographs taken from around the area, perhaps including an aerial photograph. Ask them some questions which will help them to assess the quality of their area, for example:
● Are the roads swept?
● Are the pavements safe to walk on, with no cracked paving-stones or pot holes?
● If there is a park, is it well looked after? Is there anyone or anything that spoils it?

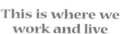
● Are the buildings clean and do they look attractive?

Move on to discuss who looks after their environment. Whose responsibility do they think it is to care for the environment? Is it just road sweepers, shopkeepers, refuse collectors, police, and so on or does everyone have a responsibility?

(40 mins) Development

Provide each child with a piece of paper to identify and describe their feelings about a place within their local environment. Ask them to complete the starter sentences: *The place I have chosen is… Things I like about it are… Things I don't like about it are… It would be better if…* Give the children five minutes to discuss what they have written in their groups.

Now ask the children to draw or paint a place where other people could relax and enjoy themselves, for example a leisure centre. Encourage them to think of things that would make it good for everyone.

(10 mins) Plenary

Invite the children to show their pictures to the rest of the class, and talk about the different places they have depicted. Have they included any special features? What are the benefits of going to their special place? How is the place cared for? Who will be responsible for looking after it? What have they learned about trying to design a special place that caters for everyone?

Differentiation

Provide less able children with a selection of pictures and ask them to make a collage which shows places where people can relax and enjoy themselves. More able children could annotate their designs and write an explanation of the decisions they have made.

Assessing learning outcomes

Are the children able to assess the quality of their own environment and appreciate elements that are beneficial to people who live there?

Vocabulary
environment
care
vandalism
value
secure
improve
damage

ICT opportunities
Create your own website about the local community, and update it regularly.

Follow-up activity
Provide the children with a list of things that they should imagine have been broken, for example a telephone box, a paving-slab, a litter bin, a shop window, a school gate, a school playhouse, a park bench, swings in a play area, a fence by a railway line, a picnic table. Encourage them to make their own suggestions. An abandoned car or a derelict factory could be included, for example. Ask the children to consider the following, working in groups: why was it useful or important in the first place? Who will be affected by it being broken? What should be done and by whom?

Building a healthy future

For children of this age, introducing them to the concept of the future may seem a somewhat over-optimistic aim, since many of them may not be either capable or disposed to thinking beyond the following day or the following week! There is, however, an important principle behind this chapter, namely the idea of getting children to think about those events or experiences which are important to them, which are milestones, times for reflection, times to look back and look forward. The process is one of developing in children their ability to reflect, to assess and also to think ahead to what is to happen to them.

Many children of this age experience the excitement of looking forward to special events, such as their birthday, a trip or Christmas. In this chapter the activities help children to use those experiences as a 'launch pad' for thinking about themselves and their growing relationships with others, as well as any hopes or dreams they may have for the future.

This chapter is also concerned with the exploration of attitudes and values. What does celebration mean? What does having a birthday mean? Perhaps it means that we can focus on the idea that we have achieved another year of growing up, learning new ways of thinking and succeeding in becoming a better person. A special event can also be a stimulus for looking forward: what do we expect to happen? What are we going to try to make happen? The classroom is an appropriate environment for the process of self-reflection to take place since it is a managed and controlled setting in which children can be encouraged to express their deeper feelings and sensitivities about themselves and others and the future.

Looking forward to…

This unit focuses on helping young children to extend their understanding of looking to the future by considering special events in the year which they look forward to with pleasure and excitement, such as birthdays or special trips. The children are encouraged to think of them not only as events in themselves but as occasions when they can think about what has happened to them in the past and what they hope will happen to them in the future.

The children are also encouraged to examine their feelings of excitement, happiness, or conversely, worry and concern, about the future. Although the children are quite young to be thinking about such issues, you can encourage them by providing them with the appropriate stimulus to look forward – thinking about a move to another class, for example, or next year when they might be moving house, or when the arrival of a baby brother or sister is expected.

Looking back on the occasion of these special events at what they have achieved is also a way of helping children to feel positive about themselves and so enhance their self-esteem. Looking forward to things which they anticipate they will achieve is a means of instilling confidence in themselves and their ability to succeed.

An important skill in looking to the future is that of planning. Initially, the children are invited to consider this in terms of planning for a holiday (activity 2). In activity 4, they are encouraged to think even further into the future, to a job which they might like to do, and consider the idea of ambition and the achievement of an important goal.

The children are encouraged in a number of these activities to draw on the experiences of parents, other relations and friends – in activity 4, for example, their parents and carers can talk to them about their work – to help them appreciate their own experiences and make sense of them.

A strong theme within this unit is that of the individual making decisions about themselves and, in the process, building up self-confidence and self-esteem. Children can be encouraged by parents and teachers to make choices, but they do not always understand what is involved in making a choice. For example, decisions are sometimes dependent upon being clear about what you want to achieve, for example *I want to be able to play the piano before I leave this school*, and having some idea of how to make a goal a reality, for example *I have to practise every night. I'll have to give up some things I like doing if that is what I want to achieve.*

The activities in this unit will enable you to try to associate in the mind of the child the idea that planning and making good choices about what they want to do in the short or medium term is about building a 'healthy' future.

UNIT: Looking forward to...

Enquiry questions	Learning objectives	Teaching activities	Learning outcomes	Cross-curricular links
Why are birthdays special?	● Share their opinions on things that matter to them and explain their views.	Children contemplating the contents of a parcel and thinking about birthdays and other special events in their lives. Paired activity in which children reflect on the year that has passed and record their ideas.	Children: ● share their opinions about events that have happened in the past and express their feelings ● talk about looking forward, in anticipation of future events ● review the past year for achievements they have made	English: describing events and experiences; compiling diary entries over a period and selecting one entry to discuss as 'special' or significant.
Why are holidays special?	● Recognise what they like and dislike. ● Recognise choices that they can make.	Whole-class discussion about holidays and times when the children are not at school. Group activity in which children complete a shared sheet, drawing items that they would take on holiday.	● talk about their feelings in association with holidays and express their likes and dislikes ● understand that holidays can sometimes be disappointing or that things can go wrong ● explain the choices that they made for their suitcases	English: role-play activity, booking a holiday in a travel agents; writing postcards about holidays. Geography: identifying chosen holiday destinations on a globe or map.
What are holidays like?	● Think about different holidays, both real and imagined, and what they are like.	Imagining holidays 50 years in the future and what they will be like. Writing a humorous story about 'my disaster holiday'.	● express their ideas about holidays	English: assembling and developing ideas.
How do you plan for a special event?	● Plan and prepare for things themselves.	Teacher-led discussion about the need for planning to make events run more smoothly. Children designing and writing a planner that they can use for a forthcoming event based on essential requirements for the day.	● understand the purpose of planning ahead ● can devise plans that could be made for a special event	English: organising and explaining information.
What will my new class be like?	● Reflect on early experiences of school. ● Predict changes related to moving into a new class and discuss them.	Children remembering their first day at school and sharing feelings about their experiences. Developing the discussion to include their ideas about moving to a new class. Group activities which involve preparing a booklet for new members of the school.	● express their feelings about their experiences of starting school or moving to a new class ● suggest appropriate ideas for giving help and advice to others	English: listening to a poem about a first day at school as a stimulus for writing about an early school memory. Art and design: recording from firsthand observation and experience.
Would I like to do that?	● Understand that they are part of a wider community in which people have different jobs.	Teacher-led discussion about the world of work. Paired activity, evaluating the merits and drawbacks of different jobs.	● give reasons for their particular preferences ● express their feelings about the prospect of future work.	English: sharing ideas and explaining their views; interviewing different adults at school in order for them to explain them jobs.

(45 mins) Why are birthdays special?

What you need and preparation
Prepare a large parcel, wrapped up as a present containing something that would appeal to the children. Collect together a variety of birthday cards showing different messages. You will also need: board or flip chart; photocopiable page 138; writing materials.

What to do

(20 mins) Introduction
Show the children the wrapped-up present. What do they think it is? Is there a clue in the way it is wrapped? What do they think is inside? When might they get a present like this? Who might it be for? Direct the children towards the idea of a birthday present and invite them to say what they would wish the present to contain. What is special about a birthday? (Note that there are religions in which people do not celebrate birthdays or Christmas, and you will also need to be aware of other festivals that children might be familiar with, such as Id-ul-Fitr or Divali.) A party or a special treat? Getting a new toy or pet? Record their suggestions on the board, then let a child open the present (to satisfy the class's curiosity!).

Now look at the selection of birthday cards together. Read some of the messages inside and compare them. Ask the children when they start to look forward to their birthday. Is it two months before it happens? One month? Two weeks? What do they particularly look forward to when they think about their birthday? Record their responses on the board. Encourage them to think about whether looking forward to an event is almost as exciting as the event itself.

(20 mins) Development
Help the children to consider what else a birthday means to them. Being a year older? A time to think about what has happened over the year? Ask the children to pretend that it is everyone's birthday today! Working in pairs, they should think about what has happened to them during the year. Were there any events which were important to them? Give out copies of photocopiable page 138 for each child to record their individual thoughts, though stress that they do not have to fill in every section if they cannot think of an idea! Explain that they are asked to include something that was disappointing to them as well as something that they enjoyed. Is there anything that they have learned? This might be a physical skill, such as learning to ride a bike, or it might be something that they have changed about their behaviour since starting school, such as remembering to share their things, to take turns, or to put things away.

Learning objective
Share their opinions on things that matter to them and explain their views.

Lesson organisation
Whole-class, teacher-led discussion; paired activities; plenary session.

Vocabulary
looking forward
wish
hope
excitement
disappointment

ICT opportunities
The children could make their own
birthday cards, to send to their friends.
Encourage them to draw their own
pictures to incorporate into their
designs.

Follow-up activities
● Ask the children to draw a special
event that took place in their lives
during the year. Their completed
photocopiable sheets ('My year that's
passed') can then be displayed alongside
their drawings.
● The children could look at horoscopes
in a newspaper or magazine and talk
about looking into the future and what
they think might happen. Encourage
them to express their opinions on
horoscopes and fortune telling. Can
they write a humorous horoscope for
each other, working in pairs?

5 mins Plenary
Invite the children to discuss what they chose to focus on in the
activity. Encourage them to talk about looking forward – is it an exciting
idea, a worry, an uncertainty? Can they tell you how far they like to look into
the future? Is it only as far as the next day or is it the next week, the next
year or a few years ahead?

Differentiation
Make sure that less able children have an adult helper nearby to prompt
them when they are working on the photocopiable sheet. Did anything
exciting happen to them at school or at home during the past year? What
can they remember? Was there anything that they did not enjoy doing?
Encourage more able children to go back further than just the past year to
look at several events or issues that were important to them.

Assessing learning outcomes
Are the children able to share their opinions about events that have happened
in the past and to express their feelings? Are they able to talk about looking
forward, in anticipation of future events? Are they able to review the past
year for achievements they have made?

50 mins Why are holidays special?

**Learning
objectives**
● Recognise what
they like and
dislike.
● Recognise
choices that they
can make.

**Lesson
organisation**
Whole-class,
teacher-led
discussion; group
activities; plenary
session.

What you need and preparation
Collect together a selection of holiday photographs. You will also need: photocopiable page
139; board or flip chart; drawing and writing materials; photocopiable page 140 (for follow-up
activity).

What to do
15 mins Introduction
Introduce the subject of
holidays by asking the children
what they look forward to most
about going on holiday. Record
their answers on the board, trying
to find common responses. Be
aware that some children may not
have had the opportunity to go on
holiday, so include some questions
about what the children like to do
when they are at home or with a
carer during the school holidays.
Encourage the children to share
their feelings about holidays –
what makes them excited, happy
or nervous? If they are going on
holiday, when do they start to think
about it? Do they feel wary about

all the travelling or the prospect of eating food that may be different from their food at home?

Use the holiday photographs to develop the idea of doing things on holiday we enjoy (or dislike!). Can they tell you whether they chose to take part in particular activities themselves? If so, did they make wise decisions? Did the activities make them feel happy? Was there anything that they did not enjoy or would not look forward to doing next time?

Vocabulary
excitement
pleasure
special
feelings
disappointment
choice

🕒20 mins Development

Divide the children into groups and give each group an enlarged copy of photocopiable page 139. Explain that they must each think of a special item that they would take on holiday, and draw it (or write the word or phrase) in the suitcase. Remind them to do this by taking turns and leaving enough room for the next person to use. They can then label the item with their name.

ICT opportunities
Ask the children to word-process a holiday list which itemises what to take and what to do!

🕒15 mins Plenary

Encourage the groups to say why the items they have chosen to go in the suitcase are special for their holiday and how it would affect their enjoyment if they went missing or were forgotten.

Talk to the children about the excitement and anticipation of looking forward to a holiday or being away from school. Is a holiday good when it actually happens or does it not match up to their expectations? Encourage them to give feedback about their experiences when things didn't go to plan. Was it disappointing? Was it funny? How did it make them feel?

Differentiation

Provide less able children with a list of items, together with key words, that they could choose from for the development activity. Encourage more able children to complete the photocopiable sheet individually.

Assessing learning outcomes

Are the children able to talk about their feelings in association with holidays and express their likes and dislikes? Do they understand that holidays can sometimes be disappointing or that things can go wrong? Are they able to explain the choices that they made for their suitcases?

Follow-up activities
● Ask the children to express their feelings about a holiday in a poem.
● Give each child a blank postcard and ask them to draw a picture on the front which shows a place that people can go to for holidays. It could be a place that they have visited themselves. Ask them to imagine that they are writing to a friend who will be going on holiday there the following week. Tell them to write on the back of the postcard about what their friend can look forward to.
● The children could role-play booking a holiday in a travel agents. Encourage the 'customers' to ask suitable questions and the 'travel agent' to describe what they can look forward to on their holiday.
● Ask the children to plan for an event – a day trip to a theme park, for example – using a copy of photocopiable page 140. Point out that they should not try to put too many things into their day (they do not have to fill something in for each time given), so that they can allow for anything unexpected happening.

1 hour What will my new class be like?

What you need and preparation
You will need: photographs of children dressed and ready for their first day at school (if available); the school's published brochure; board or flip chart; paper; drawing and writing materials.

What to do

20 mins Introduction
Show the children some photographs of children ready to start school, if you have them. Ask them what they remember about their first day at school. Remind them that it was probably a very nervous time for both themselves and their parents. Can they remember what happened? What did they like and not like? Did they enjoy their first week? Did they make friends easily? Did they like their teacher?

Encourage the children to discuss what sorts of things they would tell children who were about to start school. How could they help them to relax and not feel nervous? What did they expect to happen that didn't? Was there anything that happened that was a surprise to them?

Talk about moving to a new class – what will be new? (The teacher, the classroom, new arrangements in their daily routine, new things to learn, and so on.) What will the children look forward to most? If the children have already experienced moving to a new class, from Reception (P1) or Year 1 (P2), encourage them to discuss their experiences. If any children have recently moved to the school from another school, invite them to talk about how they felt on their first day. What sort of adjustments did they have to make?

30 mins Development
Divide the children into small groups and explain that they are going to prepare a booklet for children joining the school. Assign them different tasks, such as:
● writing and drawing about the school day – the times of different lessons and how the day is organised
● telling the reader something about the teachers and other people who are there to help them at school, such as classroom assistants, midday supervisors, and so on
● describing what sort of school clubs they can join
● drawing what the school uniform looks like (if applicable)
● explaining what they will need to bring with them on their first day.

Encourage the children to discuss any other ideas that they think would be interesting for children joining the school. These can then be included in the booklet. They may want to add their own comments about what they think of the school and what it was like for them on their first day.

10 mins Plenary

Bring the groups together and talk about the help and advice they have given. Ask them if the booklet would have helped them when they first started at the school. Look at the school's published brochure which is distributed to parents. Which parts of it do the children think are the most useful?

Differentiation

Less able children may need an adult helper to guide them when they are contributing to the booklet and to provide them with information about the school. Suggest that more able children focus on writing about their own experiences when they started school, for an appendix at the back of the booklet.

Assessing learning outcomes

Are the children able to express their feelings about their experiences of starting school or moving to a new class? Can they suggest appropriate ideas for giving help and advice to others?

ICT opportunities
Suggest that the children e-mail a school in a different area to ask pupils about their feelings and expectations regarding starting school or a new class. Comparisons could then be made to see what type of response occurs the most frequently.

Follow-up activity
Arrange for the booklet to be sent to parents of children who are going to be new entrants to the school, as a way of providing them with extra information about what life at the school is like.

50 mins Would I like to do that?

What you need and preparation

You will need: photocopiable page 141; flip chart or board; writing materials.

What to do

20 mins Introduction

Introduce the idea of the children looking for a job one day in the future. Explain that when they are at secondary school they will need to think about which subjects to study that could lead on to a job, or towards obtaining further qualifications in preparation for a job that they would be interested in.

Ask the children if they have ever thought of the job that they would like to do. Make a list on the board of their suggestions, and encourage them to give you reasons. Ask the class to respond to those who have put forward ideas – do they agree with their choice and their reasons? Would they consider doing that job themselves?

Invite the children to talk about the jobs that their parents and

Learning objective
Understand that they are part of a wider community in which people have different jobs.

Lesson organisation
Whole-class, teacher-led discussion; paired activities followed by whole-class discussion; plenary session.

Looking forward to...

other relations do. Obtain just a small sample of jobs, for discussion purposes, as you need to be sensitive to children in the class whose parents may not be working. Ask the children if they think the jobs seem appealing to them. What sorts of things do they think they would need to consider when applying for a job? (The sort of work the job entails; whether they have the necessary skills; where the place of work is and how far they will have to travel, what the hours are, and so on.)

25 mins Development

Divide the children into pairs and give each child a copy of photocopiable page 141. Ask the children to look at the jobs shown and decide if they would like to do any of the jobs in the future, using the rating scale to categorise them. Encourage them to discuss the advantages and disadvantages of the jobs in pairs, before making their decisions.

Bring the class back together and invite the children to offer their opinions. Which jobs appear to be the most popular? The least popular? Briefly analyse the choices: are there any differences between girls' and boys' preferences, for example? Discuss any interesting outcomes.

Encourage individual children to talk about their 'top job'. Why would they choose that one over all the others?

5 mins Plenary

Talk to the children about your job, why you chose to be a teacher, and about any other jobs you have done. Invite the children to ask you questions about the job.

Ask them if they look forward to the time when they will be working. Talk about the idea that quite possibly they may have a number of jobs in their lifetime.

Differentiation

Less able children may need an adult helper to talk to them about what each job shown on the photocopiable sheet involves, and to help them sort the selection, based on their preferences. Ask more able children to list on a separate sheet of paper the advantages and disadvantages that they perceive for each job, as they give it a rating. They could also add other jobs that they think they would like to do, drawing a picture for each one on the back of the photocopiable sheet, to incorporate into the activity.

Assessing learning outcomes

Are the children able to give reasons for their particular preferences? Are they able to express their feelings about the prospect of future work?

I wish I could...

This unit presents activities which allow children to think and reflect on their own personal goals and ambitions, though they require children in some cases to address these issues within the context of other people's needs and expectations. As the framework for PSHE and citizenship indicates, children should be given opportunities to understand and value themselves, and to feel positive about their lives, developing their self-esteem and confidence to become increasingly independent. This should involve children in looking at what they would like to be able to achieve both now and in the future, and how they can use their skills to meet their own needs and expectations.

Children also need to be able to understand the process of change, and to know how to cope with changes in their own lives. They need to be helped to realise that a positive attitude to change is important, as change is something that they won't be able to avoid. It is knowing how to take advantage of change that is important. Activity 2 explores this issue in the context of both familiar and unfamiliar experiences.

Within everyone there is the tendency to opt out of certain things because they don't appeal or because there is a fear of failing. Facing up to the more daunting or less pleasant aspects of our life and work can help to build our self-esteem because we know that we are coping with a part of our life that we do not like. There is satisfaction to be gained from successfully completing the difficult or the less attractive 'chores' with which we are faced. Activity 3 helps children to explore some of the strategies people adopt to avoid doing things they don't like and to examine our attitudes to responsibility and reliability. Children are also encouraged to look at this issue in terms of how it affects their relationships with others – avoidance may create short-term personal satisfaction, but ultimately end in frustration for all involved.

Giving the children the opportunity to reflect on the idea of being 'grown-up' is an important objective. Children spend a great deal of time in the company of adults, and observing their behaviour can be both illuminating and instructive! Activity 4 addresses this issue and develops tasks for the children to use in this context.

Growing up increasingly produces the unease of seeing things which we don't like, don't approve of and inevitably certain things about which we can do nothing. Helping children to cope with this kind of feeling and, equally importantly, helping them to resist the more extreme forms of behaviour that can be brought about by feelings of anger and resentment, is a vitally important role for PSHE and citizenship. Activity 5 allows the children the chance to reflect on these feelings and emotions within the 'safe' environment of the classroom, and develop a personal response.

UNIT: I wish I could...

Enquiry questions	Learning objectives	Teaching activities	Learning outcomes	Cross-curricular links
What new skills would I like?	• Develop a positive attitude about their own skills. • Know that they sometimes need to make choices about skills.	Children focusing on their individual skills and recording their ideas.	Children: • understand how their skills have developed over a period of time • have a positive attitude about their own skills • are aware that people can make choices about which skills to develop and improve	English/music/PE/Art and design: demonstrating skills to an audience.
How do I deal with change?	• Understand that people's needs change as they grow older. • Realise that learning to cope with change is important	Teacher-led discussion about the concept of change. Group analysis of different situations that involve change, including possible reactions and ways of coping.	• recognise that they are gradually changing in small ways as individuals • recognise different forms of change, and understand the importance of learning to cope with changes, whether they are for the better or not	English: sharing ideas and drawing conclusions; History: investigating changes in their own lives, the way of life of their family or others around them.
What do I try to avoid?	• Understand that avoiding doing things is not always for the good. • Realise that avoiding doing things can hurt others.	Whole-class story followed by discussion. Individuals completing a list of tasks they try to avoid doing.	• appreciate the necessity of sometimes doing things which are not very pleasurable or rewarding • appreciate that sometimes they must take responsibility for jobs, however tedious or difficult • appreciate the impact on others of not taking one's responsibilities seriously	English: using stories in shared reading to focus on the cumulative effect of neglecting to attend to menial tasks.
What's it like to be grown-up?	• Imagine what it must be like to be grown-up and think about the advantages and disadvantages.	Teacher-led discussion about being grown-up, with the children's ideas being written on the board. Whole-class story about the nature of the adult world. Group activity: children brainstorming the things adults can and cannot do, and discussing the advantages and disadvantages of being grown-up.	• perceive both the advantages and disadvantages of being 'grown-up'	English: reading stories that look at grown-ups from a different angle.
What can I do about...?	• Share their opinions on things that matter to them and explain their views. • Recognise, name and deal with their feelings in a positive way. • Recognise that certain situations, like seeing animals hurt, or property damaged, bring about different responses in different people. • Understand that expressing one's feelings about an action or situation can make people think about the consequences of that action or situation.	Teacher-led discussion about situations that are of concern because they are wrong. Paired activities evaluating different situations and the feelings they provoke; drawing scenes of situations children feel strongly about, and writing captions.	• appreciate that different situations can produce different reactions in people • express their own feelings about situations that they feel strongly about.	English: expressing own views and feelings. Geography: recognising changes in the environment and how the environment may be improved and sustained.

(40 mins) What new skills would I like?

What you need and preparation
You will need: photocopiable page 142; board or flip chart; writing materials.

What to do

(20 mins) Introduction
Remind the children of previous discussions and activities related to looking forward to new experiences, special events and being older. Discuss with them particular skills that they have developed since first coming to school. Spend some time focusing on the meaning of *skill*, the ability to do something well. Ask the children:
● Can you think of skills that you have now that you didn't have before coming to school? (Reading, writing and listening skills; playing an instrument; running, throwing and catching skills. Help the children to think about less obvious, but equally important, skills such as taking turns, making choices.)
● Which skills do you think have improved the most during your time at school?
● Which skills do you use outside school and where?
● Are there any new skills you think you will gain before the end of the year? (For example, in art or drama or using a computer.)

Invite the children to discuss the skills they admire in other people. What can they do to help themselves gain these skills?

(15 mins) Development
Distribute copies of photocopiable page 142 and read through the skills listed on the sheet. Explain that the children must choose which skills they think they have (or wish they had). Make sure they understand that there are no 'right' or 'wrong' answers.

(5 mins) Plenary
Talk about how, in demonstrating your skills and knowing that you have done something well, you can feel good about yourself. However, point out that it is important when you are good at something not to be tempted to show off or be domineering in one's behaviour towards others. As soon as you do this, and lose

Learning objectives
● Develop a positive attitude about their own skills.
● Know that they sometimes need to make choices about skills.

Lesson organisation
Whole-class, teacher-led discussion; individual activities; plenary session.

Vocabulary
grow
develop
change
skills
admire

ICT opportunities
Devise a skills checklist on a database (this could be an individual or a class list). Tick off skills when they are achieved, and add to the list as new skills are learned.

CHAPTER 5

I wish I could...

Follow-up activity
Invite the children to take part in a 'skills show' in which a variety of skills are demonstrated (use photocopiable page 142 for ideas). Encourage quieter children to participate, explaining to them that it is not a talent show and that all sorts of skills can be included, such as 'being helpful to others'.

focus on the skill itself, you may find that you are not as skilled as you thought you were! Reiterate the importance of always having time to recognise the skills of others.

Assessing learning outcomes

Are the children able to understand how their skills have developed over a period of time? Do they have a positive attitude about their own skills? Are they aware that people can make choices about which skills to develop and improve?

(55 mins) How do I deal with change?

Learning objectives
● Understand that people's needs change as they grow older.
● Realise that learning to cope with change is important.

Lesson organisation
Whole-class, teacher-led discussion; group activities; plenary session.

Vocabulary
difference
growing
improve
achieve
stronger
taller

What you need and preparation

Collect together some photographs of the school (externally and internally) taken in the past and recently, ensuring that there are changes that can be spotted easily (or you could use any building that is well-known to the children). You will also need: photocopiable page 143; board or flip chart; writing materials.

What to do

(20 mins) Introduction

Discuss the concept of change with the children. Show them the photographs of the school and encourage them to find evidence of changes that have taken place. What else do they associate with change? Is it their physical development or are there other ways in which they can change? Help them to focus on the idea that, although physically they might not be different in any way from how they were last week, they might have changed because they have learned something new. Perhaps they have learned to tie their shoelaces. This means that they are different because they are more skilful, and it is something that they have had to learn because they are growing up. Help them to understand that people are changing in small ways all the time, because they are adapting to differing circumstances that occur throughout their lives.

Encourage the children to discuss ways in which they think they have altered the way they do things recently, for example getting up earlier, exercising more frequently, changing friends. Do they think they have made changes that are for the better? Write down the children's responses, asking

them to try to explain why they have made the changes. Have they changed their opinion about anything recently? For example, *I now think that television programme is not very interesting; I don't like that piece of music anymore.*

Invite the children to talk about whether they enjoy changing things at home or at school. Talk about the difference between them changing something because they have chosen to do so and someone else changing something which affects them but without them being involved in the decision. Is that sort of change more difficult to accept? Ask them if they can think of anything in school or at home that has changed. Is it a good change? Has it affected them in any way?

20 mins Development

Divide the children into small groups of three or four and give them copies of photocopiable page 143. Explain that their task is to talk about each change listed, saying how they would be affected by it and whether they could do anything about it. If they couldn't, how could they 'come to terms' with the change? Encourage them to write brief notes on the sheet individually, once they have discussed their ideas.

15 mins Plenary

Bring the children back together and encourage them to share their responses to each changed situation. Compare the different approaches that have been taken. Talk about how it is important to deal with change positively, including those changes which we have not made ourselves and which we can do nothing about. Provide the children with a few examples, such as accepting that a person has become less friendly and kind towards you.

Assessing learning outcomes

Are the children able to recognise that they are gradually changing in small ways as individuals? Can they recognise different forms of change, and understand the importance of learning to cope with changes, whether they are for the better or not?

Follow-up activities
● Ask the children to create a poster on the theme of change, working in groups. Suggest that they make a list of points explaining why children change as they get older. They could complete the sentence: *Children change because... (they learn more things, meet more people, visit more places...).*
● Children could work in groups on presenting some form of small change in the school day to another group – their task is to persuade the others to accept it!
● Give each of the children a large sheet of paper and ask them to draw two self-portraits, one of themselves last year and one of how they are today. Can they show how they have changed? Are they bigger? Do they dress differently? Is their hair the same? What things can they do now that they couldn't do before?

45 mins What do I try to avoid?

What you need and preparation

You will need: *Farmer Duck* by Martin Waddell (Walker Books); board or flip chart; paper; drawing and writing materials.

What to do

20 mins Introduction

Introduce the idea that we all like to avoid doing certain things if we can – tidying our room, chores around the house, exercise, work that we are not interested in. Read *Farmer Duck* by Martin Waddell (Walker Books) to the children. In this story a farmer lets the duck do all the jobs around the farm while he stays in bed, reading the newspaper and eating chocolates. The duck gradually becomes so exhausted that the animals on the farm decide to take matters into their own hands. They tip the farmer out of bed and chase him away. The farmer never returns, allowing the animals to each play a crucial role in running the farm, with the tasks divided equally.

Learning objectives
● Understand that avoiding doing things is not always for the good.
● Realise that avoiding doing things can hurt others.

CHAPTER 5

I wish I could...

Lesson organisation
Whole-class story and teacher-led discussion; individual activities; plenary session.

Vocabulary
avoid
chore
responsibility
excuse
feelings
reasons
motives

Ask the children to each give one example of things they try to avoid doing. Record their answers on the board and look for common examples among them. Ask the children to give you their reasons – perhaps they get no enjoyment from the task; they cannot do it very well; it takes too long; they would prefer to do other things.

Encourage the children to talk to you about whether they try to avoid doing certain things by pretending that they are tired or ill or have got something more important to do. Remind the children that usually things they avoid doing have to be done by someone else – brothers and sisters, parents and carers. Ask how they think these people will feel towards them if they are continually avoiding these tasks.

20 mins **Development**
Tell the children that you would like them to make a list of things they try to avoid doing and to illustrate each task. They can focus on just one task, if they wish – it is their choice. If they cannot think of anything they try to avoid doing, then that is great! Instead they could consider why they are requested to carry out certain tasks that have to be done, such as looking after their clothes and belongings or feeding their pets. They can write a brief explanation and draw themselves carrying out their jobs.

5 mins **Plenary**
Talk to the children about ways in which people avoid doing certain things – not being in the right place at the right time; doing something they like instead; finding an excuse such as they do not feel well or they are too tired. Discuss the impact of 'opting out', its effect on other people. Point out that if you are unhelpful to others, then people may be less likely to help you when you need help. Finally, remind the children that unappealing tasks can leave you with a feeling of satisfaction once they have been done!

Differentiation

Ask less able children to talk to an adult helper, who could scribe their list for them before they draw their pictures. When more able children have completed the activity, and provided detailed reasons for their choices, invite them to pick one thing that they continually try to avoid doing, and to consider how they might try to make it more interesting to do.

Assessing learning outcomes

Are the children able to appreciate the necessity of sometimes doing things which are not very pleasurable or rewarding? Are they able to appreciate that sometimes they must take responsibility for jobs, however tedious or difficult? Are they able to appreciate the impact on others of not taking one's responsibilities seriously?

Follow-up activities
● Ask the children to keep a diary in which they record any changes in how they deal with 'Things I try to avoid'.
● Read the story of the lion and the mouse, one of Aesop's fables, to the children. This has the underlying moral that if you are helpful to people, they will be helpful to you in return. Alternatively, read the well-known story of the Little Red Hen, which also demonstrates the importance of helping others.
● Look at the books about King Rollo by David McKee (Andersen Press). In one story King Rollo learns the consequences of not keeping his bedroom tidy – all his toys gradually get broken until there is nothing left that he can use properly.

55 mins What's it like to be grown-up?

What you need and preparation

Take a large sheet of paper and divide it into two columns, with the headings *When you're a grown-up you can...* and *When you're a grown-up you can't...* Prepare one sheet for each group. You will also need: *Not Now, Bernard* by David McKee, Andersen Press (optional); *Drop Dead!* by Babette Cole, Red Fox (optional); board or flip chart; writing materials.

What to do

20 mins Introduction

Begin by asking the children what they think being 'grown-up' means. In what ways do they think adults are different from children? What do they think they will be like when they are grown-up? What sort of words come into their mind which would describe how they will be? Write a few words and phrases on the board that the children offer – these may be words such as *sensible, responsible, well behaved*. Include negative ideas also; for example do the children see adults as being more stressed or preoccupied than they are? At this point you could read *Not Now, Bernard* by David McKee to the children, or *Drop Dead!* by Babette Cole. Both stories can be used to give the children insights into the adult world!

20 mins Development

Divide the children into small groups to discuss the advantages and disadvantages of being grown-up. Explain that they should brainstorm ideas and write them down in the sections *When you're a grown-up you can...* and *When you're a grown-up you can't...* Tell the children that they can make humorous suggestions for either category.

15 mins Plenary

Bring the groups back together to discuss their responses. Let the class decide which ideas they think are true, which ideas they definitely do not agree with, which ideas brought out the frustrations of being a child (or an adult), which ones are the funniest...?

Assessing learning outcomes

Are the children able to perceive both the advantages and disadvantages of being 'grown-up'?

Learning objective
Imagine what it must be like to be grown-up and think about the advantages and disadvantages.

Lesson organisation
Teacher-led introduction; group activity; plenary session.

Vocabulary
grown-up
adult
responsible
behaviour
sensible
choice

Follow-up activity
Invite the children to take their group's brainstorm sheet home to gather their parents' and carers' opinions. They could see whether their ideas about what being grown-up means differ!

55 mins What can I do about...?

What you need and preparation

You will need: photocopiable page 144; flip chart or board; writing materials.

What to do

20 mins Introduction

Talk to the children about how sometimes we all see things that upset us – people being hurt, animals being mistreated, places being damaged, people's property being stolen, people behaving irresponsibly. Some of us get upset and angry when we see these

Learning objectives
● Share their opinions on things that matter to them and explain their views.
● Recognise, name and deal with their feelings in a positive way.
● Recognise that certain situations, like seeing animals hurt, or property damaged, bring about different responses in different people.
● Understand that expressing one's feelings about an action or situation can make people think about the consequences of that action or situation.

CHAPTER 5

I wish I could...

Lesson organisation
Teacher-led introduction; small group activity; paired activity; plenary session.

Vocabulary
problems
solutions
effort
collaborate
share
answers
help
co-operate

things, particularly if it affects us or someone close to us. At other times we may not feel so strongly about what has happened.

Encourage the children to discuss what sorts of actions or situations make them feel concerned or upset. Using an appropriate system of classification such as situations involving people, animals, places, possessions, write the children's suggestions on the board.

Now divide the children into small groups and give each group a copy of photocopiable page 144. Tell the children that the sheet shows a 'feelings thermometer'. (Explain what a thermometer is used for, if necessary.) Ask them to look at the different situations on the board (labelled *A, B* and so on) and rate each situation in relation to how it makes them feel, on a scale of one to ten. Encourage the children to share their 'thermometer' readings with the rest of the class. Are the results similar? Did any situations produce a rating of ten – if so, what were they and why did they make them feel that way?

20 mins **Development**
Ask the children to work in pairs to draw a scene of their own choosing which makes them angry or sad. They should then write underneath their picture a brief description of what is happening. If a victim is involved, how is he or she feeling?

ICT opportunities
The completed 'thermometers' could be reproduced on the computer using a simple graphics package, for comparison of the results.

15 mins **Plenary**
Invite the children to talk about the scenes they have depicted, and to discuss what they think could be done to prevent the situation happening again. Discuss how expressing one's feelings – for example letting someone know that what they have just done is wrong and concerns you – is very important because it can prevent the 'wrong' thing from happening again. It makes people *think* before they act.

Differentiation

Provide less able children with some examples of possible scenes, in an initial discussion, so that they can choose a scene to draw – it could be a scene showing someone throwing stones at a person's house, for example. They can then discuss their pictures with an adult helper rather than adding a written description. Encourage more able children to draw more than one scene.

Follow-up activities
● In pairs, the children could act out a situation in which one person expresses their feelings about what the other person has done, for example *I felt very angry when I saw you hit that small boy. You thought no one was looking, didn't you? I can't understand why you would want to hurt him...*
● Ask the children to produce a 'Think before you act' poster in groups.

Assessing learning outcomes

Are the children able to appreciate that different situations can produce different reactions in people? Can they express their own feelings about situations that they feel strongly about?

The squirrel in the garden

One warm, spring evening, a gardener was mowing his lawn when he spied a small squirrel scuttling along the side of a fence.

The squirrel seemed to be in a state of great excitement. As he scuttled, he flicked his tail constantly. He looked this way, then that way, as if afraid of being noticed. He scuttled some more and then stopped.

The gardener paused to watch. "I wonder what he is being so secretive about," he thought. "He certainly seems to be on a special mission."

The squirrel continued to scuttle along the side of the fence. He looked this way, then that way.

Suddenly he started to dig furiously in the soft earth between the new bright-green iris shoots.

"He has been carrying something," said the gardener quietly to himself. "What's more, he doesn't want any other squirrel to see what he is burying in that hole!"

With a final flick of his tail, another look this way and another look that way, the squirrel completed his task. He scurried up the fence and leaped into the shelter of the branches of the great beech tree next door.

The gardener waited until he was sure that the squirrel was not about to return. Quietly, he crept over to the fence and found the soft mound of earth between the fresh, bright-green iris shoots. Gently, he scraped away the earth to reveal the squirrel's secret hole. Deep in the hole something twinkled up at him – a shiny, bright-coloured marble.

PHOTOCOPIABLE

BUILDING HEALTHY RELATIONSHIPS: Being special
What is special to me? Page 8

Name _____ Date _____

My special thing

My special thing is

old

not very old

quite new

● Colour in the star that fits best.

● Make a drawing of one of your special things. Use a separate sheet of paper.

● In the empty boxes write some more words that describe your special thing.

● Colour in the one that fits best with what you do.

I like to…

hide my special thing

show it to my friends

keep it to myself

share it with my friends

● Finish these sentences.

I need to have something that is special to me because

_____

My friend has a _____ which is very

special to them. They let me _____

Name _____ Date _____

Wanted

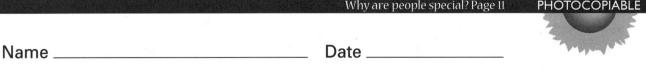

WANTED
A special person

who has these skills _____

_____

who knows that _____

_____

and who shows that they are _____

_____

Their job is to _____

_____

Name _____ Date _____

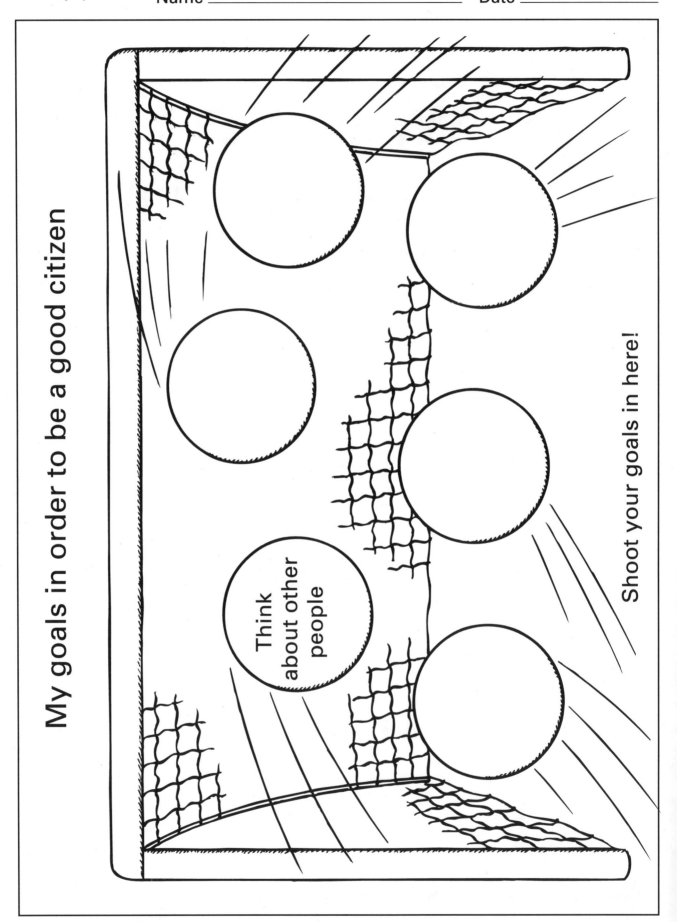

My goals in order to be a good citizen

Think about other people

Shoot your goals in here!

Name _____ Date _____

How am I special?

I am special because _____

_____

_____

I can_____

_____

_____

I know_____

_____

_____

I am_____

_____

_____

PHOTOCOPIABLE

BUILDING HEALTHY RELATIONSHIPS: Building friendships
How do I feel? Page 21

How do I feel?

I am feeling lost	**I am feeling sad**	**I am feeling uncertain/ unsure**
I am feeling confident	**I am feeling happy**	**I am feeling excited**
I am feeling lonely	**I am feeling scared**	**I am feeling angry**
I am feeling bored	**I am feeling nervous**	**I am feeling exhausted**

Name _____   Date _____

My friends

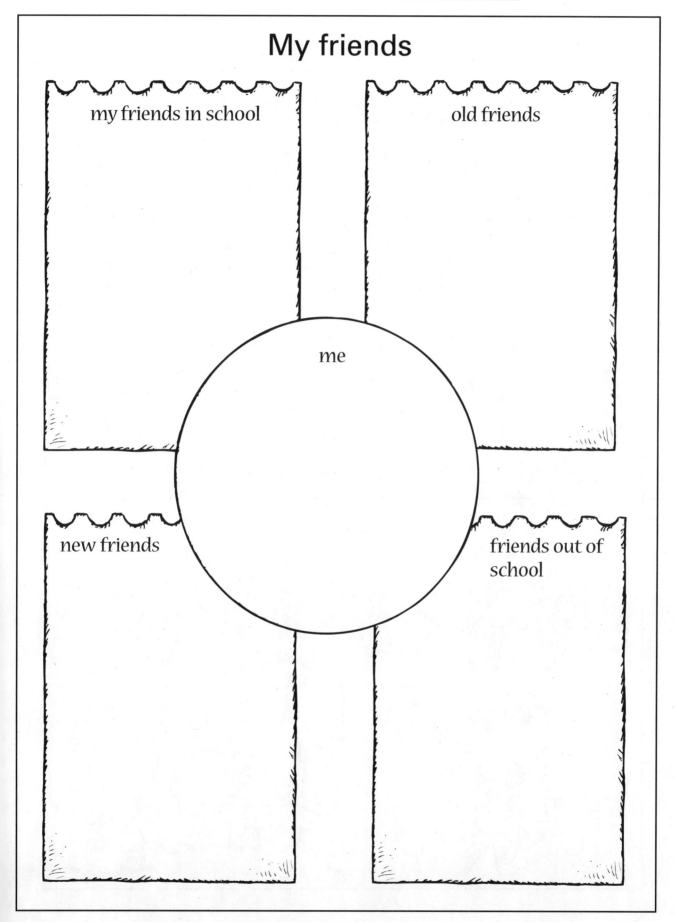

my friends in school

old friends

me

new friends

friends out of school

Friends

Name _____ Date _____

What did I do?

In this activity I...

shared

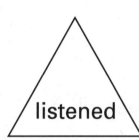
listened

was bossy

wanted to work on my own

argued

took turns

was helpful

liked working with others

co-operated

I was good at...

sharing

listening

taking turns

Name _____ Date _____

How does my body work?

Match the parts of the body to a job that they can do.

My body has...

legs to

eyes to

ears to

a mouth to

teeth to

arms and hands to

a nose to

toes to

hear what is going on around us

move where we want to go

help us to chew food

help us to see where to go

pick up and hold things

take in our food

help us to balance

help us to breathe

Name _____   Date _____

Growing up

This is me now that I am _____

I can _____

I am able to _____ on my own.

I am good at _____

I can choose _____

Soon I will be able to _____

Most of all I would like to be able to _____

_____

PHOTOCOPIABLE

BUILDING HEALTHY BODIES: My body
How do I feel about? Page 36

Name _____ Date _____

Now that I am growing up

At home, I **am** expected to _____

_____

At home, I am **not** expected to _____

_____

At school, I **am** expected to _____

_____

At school, I am **not** expected to _____

_____

My friends **expect** me to _____

_____

My friends **do not** expect me to _____

_____

Name _____ Date _____

Can you see the problems?

PHOTOCOPIABLE

BUILDING HEALTHY BODIES: What I can do for my body
What does my body need? Page 41

What does my body need?

Go to bed early	Watch too much TV
Eat lots of sweets	Eat lots of fruit
Wash their hands	Take exercise
Play outside in the fresh air	Eat breakfast in the morning
Feel good about themselves	Clean their teeth every day
Smoke	Keep clean
Travel by car	Go for walks
Eat too much	Eat lots of chips
Feel tired all day	Stay up late

Name _____   Date _____

Healthy people do this...

Never	Sometimes	Always

PHOTOCOPIABLE

BUILDING HEALTHY BODIES: What I can do for my body
How can I look after myself? Page 45

Name _____ Date _____

How can I look after myself?

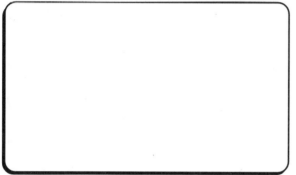

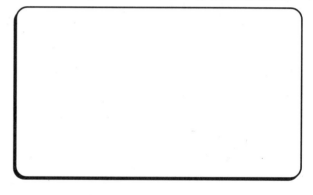

Name _____ Date _____

This is me

Me

I know my name is

_____

_____

My home

I know I live at

_____

_____

_____

Telephone number

_____

My family

Their names are

_____

_____

_____

If I got lost, I would

do this _____

_____

_____

_____

Is it safe?

Are these children taking risks?

Take care

Name _____   Date _____

Safe and unsafe

My dangerous place
Draw a place in which you might not feel safe and underneath write your reason. Say what might make that place safe.

My safe place
Draw a place in which you feel safe and underneath write your reason. Say what might make that place unsafe.

Name _____ Date _____

dangers

Keeping myself safe

risks

In the school playground I keep myself safe

by…

by not…

In the park I keep myself safe

by…

by not…

Dangers or risks

Playground: _____

_____

Park: _____

_____

Street: _____

_____

In the street I keep myself safe

by…

by not…

In the _____ I keep myself safe

by…

by not…

PHOTOCOPIABLE

BUILDING HEALTHY ENVIRONMENTS: Taking care of our possessions
What is a valuable possession? Page 63

What's the story?

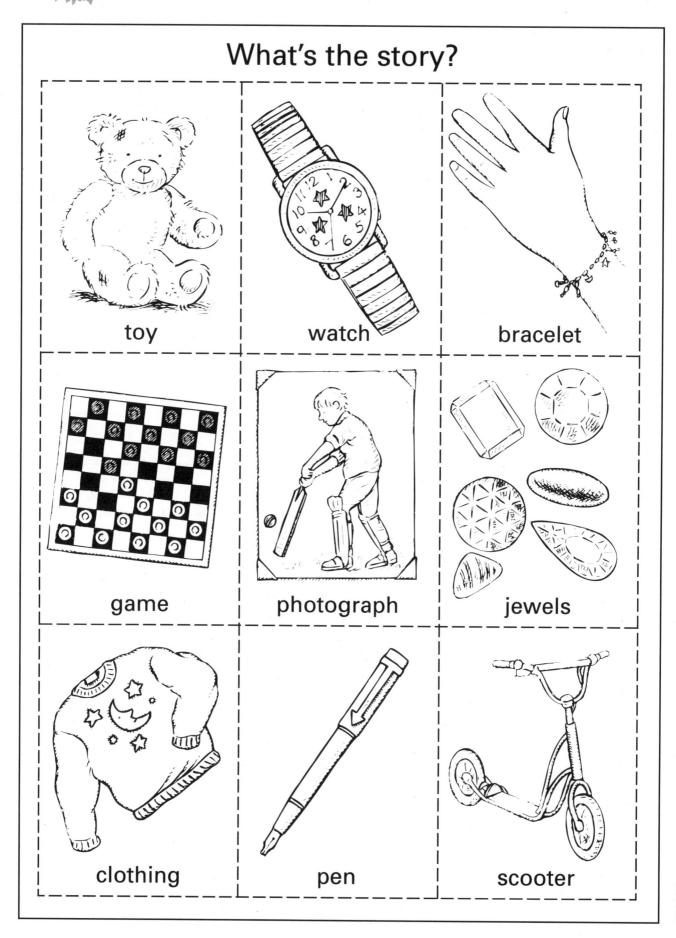

toy

watch

bracelet

game

photograph

jewels

clothing

pen

scooter

BUILDING HEALTHY ENVIRONMENTS: Taking care of our possessions

How do we look after our possessions? Page 64

Looking after our things

Think of what these people would do to look after their special possessions.

PHOTOCOPIABLE

BUILDING HEALTHY ENVIRONMENTS: Taking care of our possessions
How do we look after our possessions? Page 64

Name _____   Date _____

My special possession

I keep it in _____

_____

_____

I look after it by _____

_____

_____

Describe it

furry toy

games console

mountain bike

pet cat

doll

picture book

PHOTOCOPIABLE

BUILDING HEALTHY ENVIRONMENTS: Taking care of our possessions
What if my possessions are stolen? Page 67

Stealing is wrong

BUILDING HEALTHY ENVIRONMENTS: Taking care of our possessions

What if my possessions are stolen? Page 67

PHOTOCOPIABLE

Name _____   Date _____

Draw the story

A man looks at a motorbike in a shop window.	He thinks about how to get the motorbike. Break into the shop? Steal money and jewellery to buy it?
He breaks into a house and steals money and jewellery.	The owner of the house is frightened and upset at losing her possessions.
The man tries to sell the jewellery to get money for the motorbike.	He is caught by the police.

PHOTOCOPIABLE

BUILDING HEALTHY ENVIRONMENTS: Taking care of our possessions
Who can help? Page 68

Who can help?

teacher

parent

friend

police officer

brother/sister

neighbour

grandma/
grandpa

Problems

● I cannot find my bicycle where I left it in the park play area.

● I cannot find my watch which was a birthday present from my parents.

● I cannot find my PE bag.

● I cannot find the toy my friend let me share.

● I cannot find the change from the shopping I did at the corner shop for Mum.

Name _____ Date _____

Groups I belong to

I belong to a group with these people: _____

_____

_____

_____

_____

We are called a group because we _____

_____

_____

We get on quite well as a group because we _____

_____

_____

_____

If someone left our group, I would feel _____

_____

_____

_____

PHOTOCOPIABLE

Name _____ Date _____

Teacher for a day

Our group could take responsibility for _____

_____

_____

_____

We would do it like this _____

_____

_____

_____

We think we would be good at doing this because

_____

_____

_____

_____

_____

_____

Name _____   Date _____

Our school rules

Select two school rules and gather other classes' views about them.

Class _____	Class _____
School rule 1 _____	School rule 2 _____

_____

_____

No. of children who think it is a good (fair) rule	☐	No. of children who think it is a good (fair) rule	☐
No. of children who don't think it is a good (fair) rule	☐	No. of children who don't think it is a good (fair) rule	☐
No. of children who are not sure	☐	No. of children who are not sure	☐

Does it get broken:

very often	☐	very often	☐
quite often	☐	quite often	☐
very rarely	☐	very rarely	☐

Write your findings on the back of this sheet:
Are there any rules which they would change a little?
Should there be any new rules?

PHOTOCOPIABLE

BUILDING A HEALTHY FUTURE: Looking forward to...
Why are birthdays special? Page 93

Name _____ Date _____

My year that's passed

I remember doing these things: _____

_____

_____

I really enjoyed _____

_____

_____

I didn't enjoy _____

_____

_____

I learned to _____

_____

_____

_____

_____

Name _____   Date _____

What shall I take?

Fill the suitcase with the most important things for your holiday.

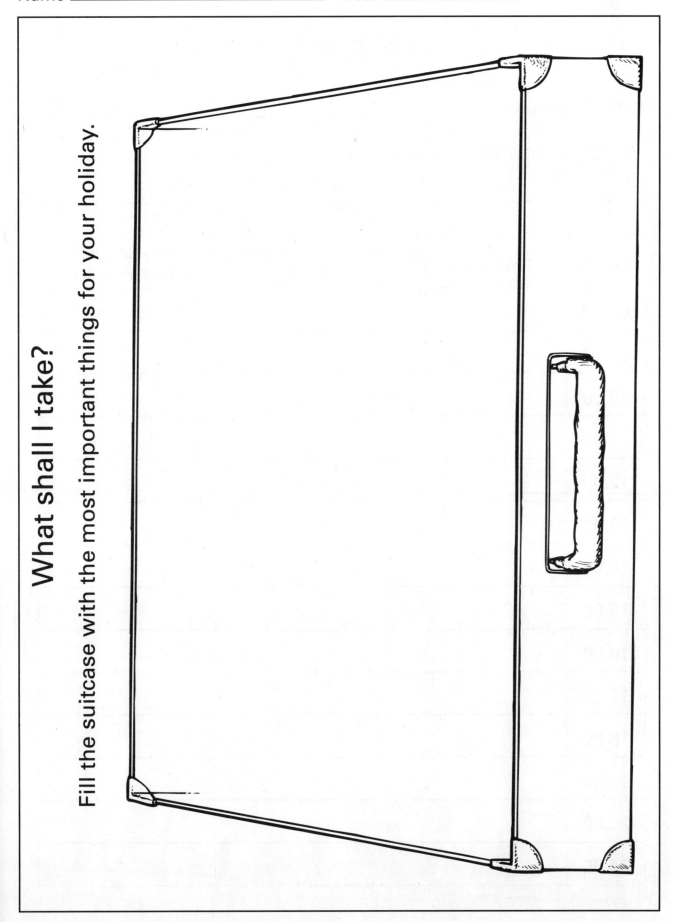

PHOTOCOPIABLE

BUILDING A HEALTHY FUTURE: Looking forward to...
Why are holidays special? Page 94

Name _____   Date _____

My planner

Name of event: _____

People who will be there: _____

_____

Times	Things to do	Help needed (if any)	Any special things required
08.00			
09.00			
10.00			
11.00			
12.00			
13.00			
14.00			
15.00			
16.00			
17.00			
18.00			
19.00			
20.00			
21.00			

Name _____ Date _____

Would I like to do that?

1 = not at all
5 = very much

Rate these jobs on a scale of 1 to 5 according to whether you would like to do them.

BUILDING A HEALTHY FUTURE: I wish I could...
What new skills would I like? Page 101

PHOTOCOPIABLE

Name _____   Date _____

My skills

Skills I have or wish I had	
Making friends	
Listening well	
Riding a bike	
Using a computer	
Keeping a secret	
Following instructions	
Being kind to others	
Drawing and painting	
Football	
Keeping my room tidy	
Dancing	
Constructing things	
Sharing with others	
Skipping	
Reading	

Choose the skills you have or wish you had.

Mark with ✓ if you think you have these skills.
Mark with ○ if you wish you had these skills.
Mark with ✗ if you do not think these skills are important.

PHOTOCOPIABLE

Name _____ Date _____

Changes

In your group talk about how you would deal with these changes.

Change	My response (Draw a face.)	What could I do about this change?
My parents are trying to get me into a new school.		
My brother wants me to swap bedrooms with him.		
My friend wants me to move to another table to work.		
My dad doesn't want me to play football with the team I'm in now.		
My parents don't want me to play at my friend's house.		

Name _____ Date _____

Our feelings thermometer

Shade in how strong your feelings are for the different situations listed on the board.

worried

disappointed

frustrated

irritated

angry

sad

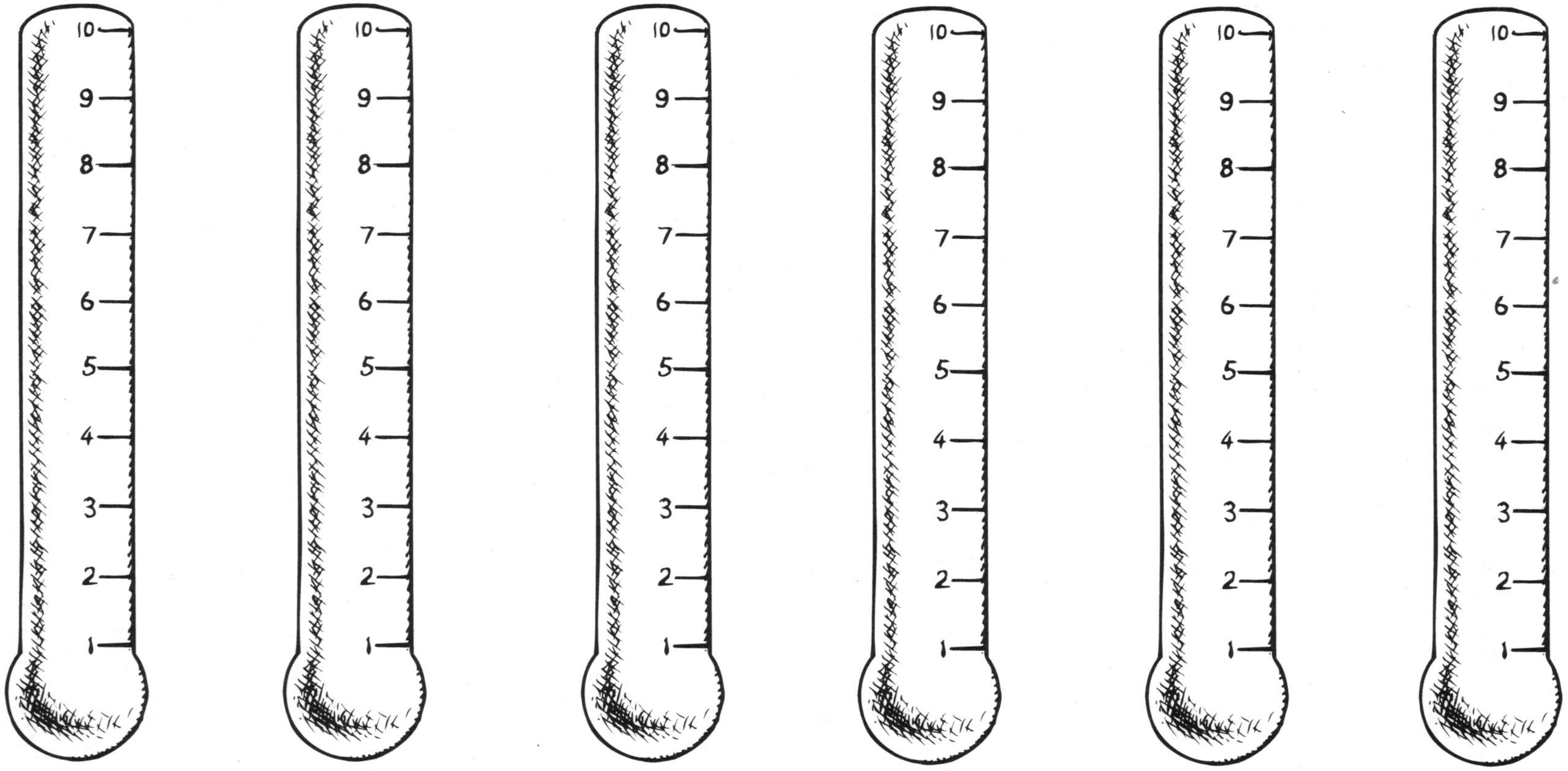